LET YOUR
LIFE
SO SHINE

The uncommon rewards

of living like Jesus

JAN PAULSEN

Pacific Press® Publishing Association
Nampa, Idaho
Oshawa, Ontario, Canada
www.pacificpress.com

Front cover photo by Ray Dabrowski, copyright © 2002
Cover and inside design by Michelle C. Petz

Copyright © 2003 by
Pacific Press® Publishing Association
Printed in the United States of America
All Right Reserved

Additional copies of this book are available by calling (toll free):
1-800-765-6955, or visiting AdventistBookCenter.com

Scripture references are from NIV (New International Version) unless otherwise marked.
Scriptures quoted from NIV are from the Holy Bible, New International Version.
Copyright © 1973,1978,1984 International Bible Society. Used by permission of
Zondervan Bible Publishers.
Scriptures marked NASB are from the *New American Standard Bible.* Copyright ©
the Lockman Foundation 1960, 1962, 1963, 1968, 1971, 1972, 1973, 1975,
1977. Used by permission.
Scriptures quoted from the NEB are from *The New English Bible.* Copyright © the
Delegates of the Oxford University Press and the Syndics of the Cambridge
University Press, 1961, 1970. Reprinted by permission.
Scriptures quoted from the NKJV are from the New King James Version.
Copyright © 1979, 1980, 1982, Thomas Nelson, Inc. Used by permission.

Paulsen, Jan.
Let your life so shine: the uncommon rewards of living like Jesus/Jan Paulsen.
p. cm.
ISBN 0-8163-1948-0
1. Spiritual life—Seventh-day Adventists. 2. Seventh-day Adventists—Doctrines.
3. Holy Spirit. I. Title.
BV4501.3 .P386 2003
248.4'86732—dc21   2002030701

03 04 05 06 07 • 5 4 3 2 1

CONTENTS

PREFACE

If you were looking for a "learned" book or a book of theology, this is not it. Interesting and enriching as the study of that is, this book is less ambitious. It seeks to share some thoughts on what happens (or should happen) when people with similar values and faith journey together through life. We relate to God and we relate to each other. We stay in touch with both. We must. Faith is meant to be very practical, as is life.

So, this book has more to do with relationships and practical elements of living as believers in Jesus Christ. It has to do with finding the richness of life in Him and in relationships that we develop along the way.

Compacted and structured as a dozen chapters on faith and living, each of them began as a sermon created in my own ministry. The publisher asked, "Can we publish some of your sermons?" Well, sermons are meant for oral delivery, with the kind of *ad hoc* elements that time and geography bring to a sermon—and occasionally with excursions from the prepared text. They are talks with the dynamics of a local situation. They don't necessarily publish well. And yet, thoughts are thoughts, and with a bit of tinkering, this is what you get.

The life of a believer should be focused on Jesus Christ. It is meant to be a safe and secure and strong kind of living. It is meant to be kind and considerate toward people. It is meant to display values that belong to Christ. It is meant to reveal a deliberately chosen goal. And it is meant to be an attractive and a good life.

May that be how we find life—and how life finds expression in us.

Jan Paulsen

CHAPTER ONE

STEADY AS YOU GO

The idea that we are "almost home" impresses on our minds images of a journey—a journey that we confess will soon come to an end. The biblical images of the Exodus from Egypt and Abraham's call out of Ur are images of God leading His people to their final destiny, to the home He has prepared for them. That will be the end of the journey. We shall then be where we were always meant to be. The goal of creation itself will then be realized.

The imagery is reinforced by Jesus when He says, " 'I will come back and take you to be with me that you also may be where I am' " (John 14:3). We are not there yet, but we are almost home. And there is an acute sense of urgency that today characterizes the church to which you and I belong. Yes, we long for the day of "arrival," but the urgency has also to do with what is happening to us, and how we spend our resources and energies on the way, as we complete the journey. And it is about this that I want to share some thoughts with you in this book. I have some concerns and maybe some wishes for what is happening, or should happen, to us as individuals and some for what is happening to us as a community, as a people.

My thoughts come in two clusters of three, considering first the individual, and later the community.

As individuals we are—most of us—certain of the Lord. He is strong, and we trust His promises; yet at the same time we are so fragile. We are fragile simply because that is our humanity. And because we are fragile we break easily, and we are hurt; and we don't know how to put together what is damaged.

- We see our fragility in the relationships we establish—or fail to establish.
- We see it in our choices of values.
- And we see it in our human tendency to keep looking back over our shoulders, sometimes wistfully because the past beckons and invites us to return, sometimes mournfully because there is so much pain associated with the past and it does not want to let go. But we do look back, one way or another, because it is so hard for most of us to be finished with the past.

In taking up these three matters of the individual, I am very much conscious of the fact that our journey is nearing its end; that there is so much to be done that requires focused energy. And I see ahead of us a whole new world—a new and wonderful future with Christ—which lies before us and invites us. So, let us consider them.

Relationships. Most of us choose our friends on a very exclusive basis. It is based on the principle that birds of a feather flock together. We feel best surrounded by people who look like us, think like us, and speak like us. And yet Jesus broke the very idea of a closed circle of friendship. He condemns everything that separates people driven by the doctrines of success—elitism, racism, nationalism, and the sense of exclusiveness that comes with them. Relationships with people are meant to be open and free, and mutually enriching, without creating dependencies, one person to another. So, if you are a thought leader, do not gather disciples to yourself. If you are "attractive," do not market yourself too aggressively. Attracting personal followers is fraught with perils both for you and them. Respect their freedom, and keep yours.

Whether we establish relationships with people or not, is not so much a choice we make. It happens just simply because we are meant to relate to each other. That is the only way to live. Loners are condemned to oblivion. So, for all practical purposes we are all involved in relationships. It is the exclusiveness of such relationships, particularly within the church, that troubles me.

So, I ask, as we are nearing the end of our journey, what is it that drives our relationships? There is obviously a sense of family among believers that brings us close to each other and holds us together. Faith in Jesus is a powerful bonding element, as is our common spiritual heritage. However, there is no place for racism, elitism, and nationalism within the family of faith. They don't belong in the church. Before Christ they stand condemned without qualification. And yet, sadly, these divisions are there. They may arise from feelings of exclusiveness, or anger, or retaliation. And these are sentiments that don't flow in just one direction.

What do we, as members of God's family, plan to do about it? It has to be resolved by the time we get to the end of the journey, for these sentiments, these distorted values, cannot be carried over the threshold into the Promised Land. As they are alien to the heart of Christ, so they don't belong in His future.

Choice of values. Every single day we are all faced with choices of values. And most of them are choices offered by the environment that surrounds us. What is the acceptable thing in my environment? The choices we make profoundly shape our lives. And they become, like it or not, value statements, for they disclose what we think is important and what we want to live for.

So we ask,

- What should I study in college, or should I just drop out of school completely?
- Whom should I marry; or, am I not the marrying kind?
- Sounds attractive, but what's in it for me?
- Shall I sell my house and move up-market?
- Should I stay where I am and work for God, or should I emigrate to America?
- Should I go for the job I was offered? The pay is a lot better and the hours more humane.
- A Global Mission volunteer? Lord, You cannot be serious!

It is late in the day, and we are almost home. And the choices we make now become very important for us personally, and for our reason for being here as God's instruments of mission. Sometimes we make stupid choices of a very personal nature and we pay for our foolishness for the rest of our lives. Sometimes, particularly when we are young, we are reluctant to stand up and take charge of our lives and make our own choices—peer pressure is hard to handle. And we delay, or vacillate, or try to stay anonymous, and in the vacuum that occurs someone else steps in and makes the choice for us and hands it to us; and it becomes so hard to say No. And therein lies the demise of many a youth to addictions of one kind or another. And sometimes we make choices in the heat of the moment that are not so much a considered choice but just happen; and we hurt ourselves and others, and we are scarred by it. We wish we could undo history, but we can't. The good news is that there is indeed a Balm in Gilead, which is still good at healing.

The question I ask is this: In making our choices—any choice—how conscious are we of the fact that we are here on a God-sent mission? How large do the facts that it is late in the day and we are here to finish God's mission loom in our consciousness as we make our choices? Says the Lord Almighty: " 'I, the Lord, have called you. . . . [You didn't call yourself; I called you!] I will take hold of your hand. I will keep you and will make you . . . a light for the Gentiles' " (Isaiah 42:6). " 'I have summoned you by name; you are mine. When you pass through the waters, I will be with you. . . . Do not be afraid, for I am with you' " (Isaiah 43:1, 2, 5). Is there a more wonderful assurance than that? " 'You are my witnesses,' declares the Lord, 'and my servant whom I have chosen, so that you may know and believe me and understand that I am he' " (Isaiah 43:10). Clearly we are here for a reason other than to eat, drink, and die.

The Seventh-day Adventist Church is not just one more sociological phenomenon. God is the cause of this church. He is in the process of completing His salvation activities, and He has chosen us for an important role in that connection. *All* of our choices must be instructed by that fact.

The inclination to look back. Whether wistfully, with a quick, backward glance, like Lot's wife, wondering if it wasn't a bit hasty to leave it all behind; or like the Israelites, remembering the "meat pots in Egypt," or as it says of the heroes of faith, "If they had been thinking of the country they left, they would have had opportunity to return" (Hebrews 11:15), many who used to be with us on this journey, regrettably, have lost their way for one reason or other. Maybe they allowed themselves to be drawn into doubts about the Christian commitment that they once made. Maybe the "longing for the better country" waned. We are not, as a church, doing enough to lovingly, caringly, and deliberately look after the needs of those who have become weary of the journey and whom we sadly do not see anymore. *Apostasy* becomes a bad word, almost like spiritual AIDS. It is as though we say, "Shame on them," or, "That's their problem." The church must accept it as our problem, and healing must be found. The cost of broken hearts in this life and loss for eternity is too high. And then there are those who keep looking back because they cannot let bygones be bygones. Haven't we all got things—events or moments from the past—that we wish were not there? But they are, and we cannot change that fact. The Lord has dealt with it and forgiven us, other people have forgiven, but somehow we find it so hard to forgive ourselves. And it becomes a plaguing memory that denies us the joy and sense of security we should have as we finish the journey. And it is a failure of faith.

It is not the flawlessness or perfection of our lives that is the critical factor, but the role of Christ in our lives and the unqualified decisions we make for Him. There is then no need to look back. Individually and as a people our eyes are to be fixed on

- the goal of our journey,
- the One who is going to take us there, and
- what must engage and occupy us until we are there.

With an eye to us as a community, I have three main concerns—or maybe *ideals* is a better word—which I feel strongly for. They fall into three categories: mission, quality of life in the church, and unity.

Mission. The comprehensive message of the Bible is that humanity's lost condition and hopelessness can only be resolved by God, and God has chosen to do that through Jesus Christ; and, in fact, that is the only way it can be done; *and* that the church is God's selected instrument to carry that good news to people. The Bible spends very little time speculating on the success or failure of individual mission activities. It just says, "Do it!" Or, in the parting words of Jesus, " 'You will be my witnesses . . . to the ends of the earth' " (Acts 1:8). That means simply everywhere! We have no other reason for being! That is why we are.

As we all know well, we human beings establish organizations—societies, clubs, fraternities, lodges, and what not—in order to care for the interests of those who are members, who have paid their dues and are in regular standing. The church is different. God established it primarily in the interest of those who are not members. It is important for the church to remember that and not become too preoccupied with itself or feel too special on its own. It is the world of fallen sinful people that God loves, and He needs the church to communicate that truth by words and deeds. "The burning, consuming love of Christ for perishing souls is the life of the whole system of Christianity" (Ellen G. White, *Lift Him Up*, p. 134).

The very simple message that comes from a quick look at Israel of old is that God's choice of them as a nation was for mission and witness. When Israel withheld that service, the nation's status lost its meaning. When God caused this Advent movement of ours to come on the scene of history some 150 years ago it was for us to be the carriers of a particular focus on Scripture that God wanted men and women to know about at this end time in history. And much of that is contained in our understanding of eschatology, the teaching of the earth's last events and the final stage of earth's history. And that is where we are in time today.

God's love for humanity is broad and comprehensive, and it includes you and me. But we are particularly useful to God as the carriers of His mission. So all that we are and have as a church finds its meaning in mission. I therefore ask that all initiatives we as a church engage ourselves in be identified and defined in terms

13

of mission. So I say to my colleagues in leadership and planning: "Make a note of that." Our strategic planning is for mission. Our use of resources is for mission. And if we don't see the linkage between what we do and mission, we must ask, Why do we do it? Should we not be doing something else? For it is late in the day, and we are almost home, and we must not now become distracted.

The quality of life in the church. The truly wonderful thing about Jesus Christ is His immeasurable love for people—individuals who are disfigured, scarred from the battles of life, "smelly," ill-tempered, and cantankerous! But wonderfully loved by our Lord! Just by belonging to humanity we are highly valued by Him. We don't have to become anything or achieve anything to be loved by Him. And being highly valued by Him is not something that comes at an advanced stage of life when we can display a good track record that testifies to the fine "stuff" of which we are made. Each of us has that intrinsic value simply by being a human being. And as such we are deeply loved by God. Is your and my local congregation able to communicate that? Is this the aura that comes from our churches? Can someone walk off the street into your local church and feel the atmosphere of openness and warmth and loving acceptance?

> The people of the world are looking to us to see what our faith is doing for our characters and lives. They are watching to see if it is having a sanctifying effect on our hearts, if we are becoming changed into the likeness of Christ. . . .
>
> It is not the opposition of the world that will most endanger us; it is the evil cherished right in our midst that works our most grievous disaster. . . .
>
> There is no surer way of weakening ourselves in spiritual things than to be envious, suspicious of one an-

other, full of faultfinding and evil surmising (Ellen G. White, *That I May Know Him*, p. 153).

Memory takes me back to a local church in which I worshiped years ago. Among those who came was a young teenager. He came reluctantly, he came late, and he would walk in after the others—those were his choices; and he sometimes came in jeans; that was also his choice. He carried anger against the church and the Lord; and there were things happening around him that he found difficult to understand and accept. He was a hurting and unhappy young man. His appearance irritated one of the local church elders; maybe he dressed so as to make sure he would irritate him. One day the elder said to him: "Go home and change before you come back." He went away, and to this day, many years later, he has not come back.

Just like our Lord, the church must be in the "business" of saving people. That is where our whole existence is summed up! So, when you define your church, your local congregation, culturally and in other ways, just be sure that it remains good at saving people. For if not, we may have saved a structure and an organization, even a reputation, but we are no longer useful to God.

Unity. Whilst our rapid growth is a wonderful thing and a tribute to the God whom we serve, the very size, internationality, and cultural, political, and ethnic diversity of our church poses a formidable challenge in terms of unity. As a world family we are different from every other church. We are not a fraternity of similar national churches. *We are one!* There are a number of elements of unity that are unique to us:

- We have one set of fundamental beliefs.
- We have one common Church Manual.
- We have a common constitutional structure and similar policies.

15

- We are financially "intermarried" and we share our resources around the world.
- We have one shared sacred gift in the inspired writings of Ellen White.

These are God's gifts to us. So, it is not just "by our love that they shall see that we are one." There are a number of tangible elements of unity that uniquely bind together as one this family around the world.

Unity, however, does not look after itself. Hence the injunction: "Make every effort to keep the unity of the Spirit" in the one body (Ephesians 4:3).

And some of us don't!

I recognize that as this church grows around the world, the local needs of the churches will also grow. The local needs will be financial, and there will be needs in terms of how the church should function and express herself. I understand that we should examine how these local needs can be met. I understand that in the process of doing so we will ask ourselves: What changes can we safely make? Changes with regard to how we share and use our money? Changes with regard to how ministry functions? Changes with regard to the structures of administration in our church? I understand the need for these questions to be asked and explored. In answering them, however, it is important that leadership does not sacrifice what binds us together worldwide.

There is something profoundly biblical about being willing to forego one's local exercise of freedom in the interest of what is good for the whole international Adventist family. We owe it to *Christ,* whose idea it was that has brought us to where we are today, to be very deliberate and careful in holding the family together.

It is late in the day, and we are almost home. We cannot now become reckless and careless. We owe it to the church, which is His body, to shore up and strengthen the whole body—the international family. In this context "congregationalism" does not belong; it is an alien concept that is irreconcilable with what God has given to this church. It is critical that elected leadership accepts this and discharges its leadership in harmony with what God has given to us.

So I say to the elected leadership: "Don't undo the elements that bind us together—the agreements we have arrived at as a spiritual family!" And I say to the rest of the church: "Hold your leaders accountable."

This is my vision of the church:

- I see the Seventh-day Adventist Church as God's redemptive community in these last days.
- I see it as an open and seeking community, and I believe we bring to the world a very particular focus on the Word of God.
- I see Christ as our Savior, Friend, and soon-coming Lord.
- I see the Seventh-day Adventist community as one united family in which the blend of all cultures and races enrich our quality of the life we share.
- I see this community as a mission instrument for God.

Can each of us look at this description and say: "Yes, that's my community; this is my people; that's where I belong; this is my spiritual home"? If you can say "Yes," I want you to feel safe and loved and at home in this church. I pledge to do what I can to make our church a loving community in which we support each other—carry each other, if need be—lift up our Lord, and seek to live our lives in obedience to Him; and arrange our lives, values, and choices, personally and in the church, accordingly.

Now, let us embrace and hold hands firmly, let us "press together," as we move forward to finish the journey!

CHAPTER TWO

ARMED WITH THE POWER OF THE SPIRIT

Luke 24:36-49; John 14:25, 26

Throughout Scripture one of the striking features of the coming of the Holy Spirit to the believers is that He comes with *power.* Not power in the sense of authority of office or position, but in the sense of ability to perform, to function, to act, to do something special, and to enable a person to become something that before he was not. Something out of the ordinary happens!

Immediately before Jesus was taken up into heaven He said to His close disciples: " 'You will receive power when the Holy Spirit comes on you; and you will be my witnesses . . . to the ends of the earth' " (Acts 1:8). And this statement immediately begs the question: Wherein lies this power? What is it?

To get our minds in focus to what we are going to talk about, look at a few examples from Scripture:

John the Baptist. It was said of him that " 'he will be filled with the Holy Spirit even from birth. Many of the people of Israel will he bring back to the Lord their God. And he will go on before the Lord, in the spirit and power of Elijah . . . to make ready a people prepared for the Lord' " (Luke 1:15-17).

Mary. The angel said to her, " 'The Holy Spirit will come upon you, and the power of the Most High will overshadow you' " (Luke 1:35).

Jesus. After He was tempted for forty days by the devil in the wilderness, the Bible says that "Jesus returned to Galilee in the power of the Spirit, and news about him" spread everywhere (Luke 4:14). And Peter, in one of his powerful sermons, spoke of this remarkable presence of power in Jesus. He said: "You know what has happened . . . how God anointed Jesus of Nazareth with the Holy Spirit and power, and how he went around doing good ... because God was with him" (Acts 10:37, 38).

Paul. He described his own ministry as being "sanctified by the Holy Spirit," and, therefore, what he was doing and saying was done "through the power of the Spirit" (Romans 15:16, 19). And, says Paul, "our gospel came to you not simply with words, but also with power, with the Holy Spirit" (1 Thessalonians 1:5).

The church. And of the church herself it is said that you will be armed with power from above " 'when the Holy Spirit comes on you; and you will be my witnesses' " (Acts 1:8). And when the first believers were brought before the Sanhedrin, the question put to them was: " 'By what power or what name did you do this?' " (Acts 4:7).

It is clear that the coming of the Spirit is associated with power. Having the Holy Spirit gives us a powerful Companion; the Spirit's presence means access to power.

Wherein lies this power? What is it?

The power of the Holy Spirit is first and foremost the power of *creation*. It is the ability to take what is really nothing and make something useful of it, something wonderful and something of great beauty! It is the power to make something that is neither the rational, nor the logical, nor the natural consequence of anything that was before. It is *new!* It is wonderful. That is the power of the Spirit, and precisely for that reason He was in early Christian literature described as the "Creator *ex nihilo.*"

And you see this from the very beginning of time in the Creation story. The Spirit is there "hovering over the waters" (Genesis 1:2), light pushing aside darkness so that all kinds of things could be seen to emerge.

Where did these things come from? They have no "natural" origin in creation. Plants, animals, birds, even man—in a sense they came from nowhere. The "dust of the earth" is not our natural origin; and the book of Genesis is not a textbook on how to make things. It is a faith testimony to the God who makes out of nothing. He is there; and it happens. The same thought is captured in Job 34:14, 15: The Spirit is there, and it happens; the Spirit is gone, and " 'mankind would perish.' "

God makes life, He gives life, He keeps life, and He renews life. We never own life. It is the property of God; and without His Spirit there is no life. That is the simple but powerful assertion of the Word of God.

The same Creator Power is seen in the Spirit as the Creator of a new people. Notice in the poetic language of Isaiah how the parched and barren comes alive with the Spirit:

> "I will pour water on the thirsty land, and streams on the dry ground; I will pour my Spirit on your offspring, and my blessing on your descendants.
> They will spring up like grass in a meadow, like poplar trees by flowing streams" (44:3, 4).

And that is the same thought captured by Ezekiel in the vision of the dry bones (see chapter 37). The setting for this scene is that of the Israelites searching for a future from the bleakness and barrenness of captivity in Babylon. Would they be alive again as a nation? And in answer to their searching comes this vision of the dry bones. There was no life in the bleached bones. They are symbols of utter lifelessness. God says, " 'I will put breath [my Spirit] in you, and you will come to life. Then you will know that I am the Lord' " (Ezekiel 37:6, 14). They were to come alive again.

It is the Spirit that makes the difference. Out of that which is not, the Spirit makes something. The Spirit brings the sparkle back to life. And, said the text, what you discover when the Spirit enters your life is that He is the Lord. It is Christ, the Lord and Savior, who jumps into focus. The Spirit's presence has to do with Christ as Lord and Savior. It does not have to do primarily with "speaking strange tongues," swaying in the wind of some rhythmic music, or performing some strange act that fools the senses. No, the Spirit's presence immediately acknowledges Jesus as Lord and Savior and leads to a life with Him.

The same creative power of the One who "creates out of nothing" is seen in the conception of Jesus (see Luke 1:35). Please, don't try to explain it logically because it is illogical, not rationally because it is irrational, not naturally because it is unnatural. It all points to the fact that there is a world beyond our normal reach, beyond what we can normally see, recognize, and do; and that is the realm where the Spirit reigns. The Spirit has the capacity to take us beyond ourselves. Where there is no life, there shall be life. That is the wonderful assurance we are given! Listen to the words of the prophet Isaiah:

On the land of my people will come up thorns and briers . . .

Until the Spirit is poured upon us from on high, and the wilderness becomes a fruitful field. . . .

Then . . . my people will dwell in a peaceful habitation, in secure dwellings (32:13-18, NKJV).

And the same creative power is seen at Pentecost, when a wholly new community is created. That small group of believers had come out of the Easter weekend confused, discouraged, and dismayed at what had happened. Now we see them as men and women of strength, full of courage, confidence, commitment, and hope, and certainly not afraid to show their identity. But more important, they emerged as a people *able to witness.* What made the difference? The power of the Spirit.

As confused and discouraged men and women we cannot witness for the Lord. *Confusion* means that we have nothing to say, we have no message to bring. *Despair* means that we have no power with which to deliver it. Whatever we have to say is weak, insipid, and feeble.

As Christ was bodily taken up to heaven, a new "Body of Christ" emerged: The church. The coming of the Spirit signifies a renewal (see Titus 3:5).

What does all of this say to us now? What can the presence of the creative power of the Almighty God do to us? What is it meant to do to us?

It is first and foremost something very personal in our lives. The presence of the Holy Spirit is meant to bring Christ into focus. In promising the Spirit Jesus said that when He comes He would help you to understand Him. Said Jesus, " 'He will bring glory to me by taking from what is mine and making it known to you' " (John 16:14). And, said Jesus, " 'Then you will know the truth, and the truth will set you free' " (8:32). The freedom of which Jesus speaks is nothing other than a "not guilty" verdict. Knowing Jesus as a Friend, as a life Companion, as Lord and Savior, as the Healer of broken hearts and broken lives— knowing Him takes care of everything!

This is what Paul means by justification. He compares the entering of the Spirit into one's life with the freeing of a slave from all his fears. The Spirit assures us inside that we are God's children (see Romans 8:15, 16, cf. Galatians 4:6, 7). And you can shout out: "I am not a slave to sin; I have been set free; I am a child of God; I am an heir to the kingdom." For "where the Spirit of the Lord is, there is freedom" (2 Corinthians 3:17). And this is not a promise for some distant future; it is a reality now! It brings an incredible sense of revival and renewal.

The Spirit's presence also helps us to discover the meaning of prayer; He helps us to enter into a dialogue with God. He helps me to know God not as a distant and mysterious ruler who is to be feared or even ignored because we know so little about Him. The Spirit's presence helps me to know Him as my Father; a Father who is deeply involved in my life and who cares about what happens to me. So many lives fall apart; so many human beings destroy themselves because they believe that no-body cares. GOD CARES! We are sometimes so distressed by the pains of life that we dare not hope, and we don't know how to pray; and we feel so weak, and the future is so uncertain. The Spirit helps us in our weakness to pray and "intercedes for us" before God the Father (Romans 8:26). He brings to us the as-surance that we are God's children. The Spirit confirms with our inner spirit that even now we are His (see Romans 8:16). This brings a new quality to our lives—a sense of being safe!

The Spirit's presence leads us to live lives of holiness. God says to us: "I want to put My stamp, My identity, on your lives. I want it to be visible that you are Mine. I want your values in life to reflect that you are Mine. I want your choices to be Mine. I want your life to be different because you are Mine, and because I have given you both the reason and the power to live differently."

Since the Spirit is with you, says God, I want you to "keep in step with the Spirit" (Galatians 5:25). In this chapter of Galatians Paul contrasts the life of the Spirit with the life of the flesh. Well, says Paul, you cannot be sowing the seeds of the sinful flesh and expect to reap the fruit of the Spirit! It is just not going to happen. And he is very explicit in what he is talking about. He lists the fruits of both kinds of life. There is no reason to be vague or ignorant about these things. God contrasts two different types of life. And the Spirit makes the difference. It is the Spirit that sanctifies (Romans 15:16).

The Spirit leads to certain fruits being in evidence—or "fruit of the Spirit." The list is specific and each of the fruits shapes our lives. The fruits are love, joy, peace, patience, kindness, goodness, faithfulness, gentleness, and self-control. They all have in common that they cannot be harvested in a private, secluded, and isolated life; they find their meaning only in relationships with people. This has to do with being a better person to be around. It has to do with being sensitive and considerate toward other people. It has to do with understanding them, their needs and their burdens, and not just expecting to be understood ourselves. It has to do with not hurting or destroying other people.

Have you paused to reflect on what will bring people into the church, and, once they are in, what will keep them there? Whilst it is true for many that it was doctrines and lifestyle values that brought them into the church, very few people have left the church because their acceptance of the doctrines collapsed. No, they left because of some personal hurt, or because someone inside the church failed to share with them the fruits of the Spirit. Rather, they encountered someone who was destructive, who deeply disappointed them, or who caused them hurt that somehow they could not find healing for. And so they are gone.

We cannot read the Gospels without being struck by the fact that it matters very much to Jesus Christ how we treat people. The sad fact is that many are walking away from Christ and the kingdom because they have found life so offensive and destructive in the presence of some other "believer." When that happens, the presence and power of the Spirit is being denied. We are here talking about qualities of life that Christ wants His people to discover and develop. They say much about what God wants His people to be like.

The unity of the Body of Christ that Jesus wants for His people is made possible by the presence of the Spirit (see Ephesians 4:3, 4). This unity is not essentially made possible by consensus statements, by agreed formulas, or by policies. They may all express this unity and serve to keep it functioning, but the unity of the family of God is primarily a product of the creative presence of the Holy Spirit. He is the One who bonds the members of the family together. Christ wanted them to be one. He prayed that " 'they be brought to complete unity' " (John 17:23). By the symbolism of the body He has modeled how it is to work (see Ephesians 4). And as a church family God gave us early in our history a working model of how this unity is to be developed organizationally around the world.

The Spirit's presence makes *evangelism and witness* possible. You can tell interesting stories and be an entertaining speaker by your own wit and charm, but you cannot bring the gospel of salvation without the Spirit's presence and power. He is the One who takes the words of men and women and fills them with life! That is why Jesus' parting words to His disciples were: " 'Stay in the city until you have been clothed with power from on high' " (Luke 24:49). The Spirit makes the difference.

This is clear beyond any shadow of a doubt: the Spirit's creative presence is the catalyst to achieve (1) the desired quality of life; (2) unity in the family of faith; and (3) growth—both as evangelism and as personal inner growth of faith. Without the Spirit none of this will happen!

And so the question remains: Where do we go to find this power, this Spirit? Is it a hidden mystery? Is the Spirit an elusive promise for some uncertain future? Can anyone—can I get that power now?

I know there are some who pray for the "latter rain" of the Spirit as though the Holy Spirit is a stranger to the church now. I am here to tell you today that He is here among us. The Spirit has come. When you gave your life to Christ and made your commitment to live a life with Him as Lord, He in response gave you a gift. Actually, Paul states it very strongly: When you accepted salvation in Christ "you were marked in him with a seal, the promised Holy Spirit" (Ephesians 1:13). So, something has already happened, a "first installment" of what is to come.

The question is much more: What are we doing about it? Are we living lives of the Spirit, or are we living lives of denial? Are we allowing the potential of the Holy Spirit's presence to find full expression in our lives? Or is it possible that that power is being suppressed or denied? That we are actually robbing ourselves of richness that could be there—of a quality of life that Christ wants us to have already now?

Please note what the Lord's servant has to say in commenting on what the Holy Spirit can do through us as stewards of God. She writes:

> Lessons need to be learned by all who shall step into places where they are to be proved and tested by God. . . . The creating, transforming power of God's Holy Spirit

will make them copartners with Jesus Christ. Yoked up with Christ, they can be more than conquerors through Him (Ellen G. White, *Testimonies to Ministers and Gospel Workers,* p. 328).

And,

The promise of the Spirit is not appreciated as it should be. Its fulfillment is not realized as it might be. It is the absence of the Spirit that makes the gospel ministry so powerless. Learning, talents, eloquence, every natural or acquired endowment, may be possessed; but without the presence of the Spirit of God, no heart will be touched, no sinner be won to Christ. On the other hand, if they are connected with Christ,* if the gifts of the Spirit are theirs, the poorest and most ignorant of His disciples will have a power that will tell upon hearts. God makes them the channel for the outworking of the highest influence in the universe (Ellen G. White, *Christ's Object Lessons,* p. 328).

The message is simple: God has the power to change our lives. He can do it, and He longs to do it. And the power to accomplish it is here now. Without it we cannot be united as a church, we cannot grow—personally and as a community—and without it we cannot reach the kind of quality of lives that He desires for us. So, what shall it be? Whether it will happen is for you and me to decide.

---

* "Connected with Christ" means access to the power of the Spirit.

CHAPTER THREE

A BIT OF ADVENTURE

John 21:15-18

As I picked up the telephone I recognized the voice imme-diately. This time it came from San Jose, Costa Rica. This is what it said:

"I have just returned from Colombia. Some of our aid programs take us to regions outside the control of the central government. You walk up some streets and you see kids, twelve- and thirteen-year-old boys, with the latest automatic weapons. A look into their eyes tells you that their minds have been blown away with drugs. I was taken to a shack where a mother sat weeping at the bedside of her son who was wounded by gun shots. He was dying, and she had nowhere to take him."

Two months later the same familiar voice reached me, as it had many times in between, but this time from Kigali, Rwanda:

"I have just come out of Goma, the notorious refugee camp in Congo. The situation there is beyond description. It is starving hell for the kids. Did you hear of the six Red Cross workers who were killed this week in Congo?"

I told him that I had; I had just heard it on the news.

"Well," he said, "two of them were colleagues with whom I was working. We are all shocked, and apart from feeding the refugee children we have all gone on strike for a week."

So I said, "Are you sure you ought to be doing this?"

He said, "Dad, you and Mom need to remember that this is my free choice; relief and development aid work is my profession. This is my mission, this is what I want to do."

Is there room for some adventure in your plans?

Once you have met Jesus Christ and you have accepted His offer of friendship, and you have started your Christian journey with Him, is that all there is to it?

Once you have your basic doctrines sorted out, and you have settled into a steady-as-you-go church life, with victories slightly outnumbering defeats, is that it? Is there nothing more? I mean, is there no excitement beyond that? Isn't there a bit of newness and adventure still to be had in your life with Christ? Or is it enough for you to have got your definitions of faith right, your health formula professionally verified, and are giving your tithe and offerings? Does that capture the essence of what your life as a Christian is going to be like?

One does not travel very far in life before one discovers the unevenness of life. You get out of bed on one side one morning and life is wonderful. You try the other side the next morning and discover that life is not very fair at all, that it can be brutal. And believing in God does not make it any fairer. Illness and accidents, death and misfortunes, blessings and curses come randomly, unpredictably, and so often unfairly. These are some realities that may make you weep bitterly, but which you can rarely protect yourself from.

And you may look at life and say: How can I find a formula for a "good" life, mostly safe, but also interesting? Is there such a formula? Well, probably there is, especially if you don't make it too complicated. Allow me to make some suggestions.

1. Acknowledge Jesus Christ as Lord, and make the decision that allows Him to build and shape your life.
2. Do what you *know* is right. In most situations we know what is right and what we should do, but our decision-making mechanism gets crowded by a heap of not-so-pure ulterior motives. And we make decisions that we live to regret.
3. Check your basic attitude to people. Be *kind,* be generous.
4. Try to be *creative* and a bit *adventurous.*

Each of these can be dwelt on lengthily, but it is this last one that I want to invite you to think about a bit. And I would do so asking you *not* to think first and foremost about making money, about graduate school and elaborate professional plans for the future. Don't be in a hurry to make money, or get locked too early into a professional pattern from which there is no escape! But consider giving yourself some months or a year to do something creative and adventurous for the Lord, and in the process learn to know the world and the people who live in it, and know the internationality of the planet on which you have been placed and which you have been asked to look after. Go to Africa or to one of the islands of the South Pacific, or to Asia. Be a volunteer in some special project where you *give* to make the lives of others better and more promising; learn to live very simply with very little spending money; and come close to the earth and to people. And you will discover the immeasurable value of human beings, and why God loves them.

It is not a life without danger, but it is education that you cannot obtain any other way.

The life of the apostle Peter gives us some insight into the delicate growth of a person from where one starts to where one needs to be going—what he discovered as he stepped out from what he was doing. (And it is of course the Holy Spirit that takes one along that journey.) Peter discovered early in his walk with Jesus an unquenchable thirst, an unstoppable craving, for something more, something richer, something deeper in his life with Jesus. It was like the love between a man and a woman which is stable and strong, and yet is constantly seeking greater closeness and understanding, a growth in refinement which increases one's sensitivity to the signals of one's partner. Whatever there is, it is never enough; love is constantly seeking for more.

We know very little about Simon Peter before Jesus met him. But we know that he came from Bethsaida, a fishing village on the northern shore of Lake Galilee. He was a fisherman by trade, an unschooled and ordinary man, honest and hardworking. By temperament he was spontaneous, he was a bit impetuous, and he triggered easily.

And then along came Jesus of Nazareth.

Simon was instantly drawn to Jesus. The text says that "at once" he left his fishing nets and went with Jesus. Maybe fishing is not the ultimate professional fulfillment in life, but even so . . . Or maybe he felt the strength of His character, or he just happened to like Him. In any case there was something in Jesus that drew Peter and pulled him away from anything else.

Jesus was transparently honest. He had remarkable insight. He read you like an open book; and He had understanding for your inner struggles. He was remarkably generous. He expressed His views without fear. This man, Jesus of Nazareth, was different. Peter saw that He had power over the wind, the sea, over illnesses and deformities, over evil and demons. Oh, this was quite magic! He could pull a crowd all right, and Peter felt himself drawn into this circle. And he began to walk with Jesus.

There are some radical choices that you must allow your-selves to make in life. Let Him take you on roads you may not otherwise choose to travel.

At one time, as Jesus noted that there were some to whom the price of discipleship had become too high and they had left and just disappeared, Jesus asked His closest disciples: "Are you also going to leave?" Peter was the first to answer: "Where should we go? [Where do you go if you turn your back on Him?] You are the only One who has the words of eternal life" (see John 6:67, 68).

Look at what happened to Peter on his journey with Jesus. The first incident happened on the road to Caesarea Philippi when Peter, in response to Jesus' question about whom they said He was, said: " 'You are the Christ, the Son of the living God' " (Matthew 16:16). Notice what Jesus said to that. He didn't say: "Now, that's a smart fellow. Well done! What have you been reading of late?" He said, "Simon, this is not something that you have worked out for yourself, nor is it something you have been taught by other men. It has been revealed to you." And suddenly a new dimension of knowledge and understanding is being introduced to Peter, and to all followers of Jesus: *revelation*. The touch of God! Which is God's way of saying to a person, "I am here. This is what I have to say to you."

By the touch of God the first thing Peter sees is Jesus. Not Jeremiah, or Elijah, or anyone else. They are history, *but Jesus is special!* And that personal discovery of the identity of Jesus from now on begins a process of transforming Peter.

Your personal discovery of the identity of Jesus is what matters! Not the discovery that your parents made, not the wording of a particular statement of belief, not the formula of something a teacher taught you in the classroom, not a memory text from the distant past. Yes, all of this may well be part of it, but we are here talking about something very personal. It is a discovery of something important that *you yourself* have made. And it is the Holy Spirit who helps you to find out who Jesus is (1 Corinthians 12:3). Said Jesus: " 'You will know the truth, and the truth will set you free' " (John 8:32); and " 'I am . . . the truth' " (John 14:6). To discover for myself the identity of Jesus Christ is revelation. "It has been revealed to you," said Jesus. Revelation is the touch of God. And with that discovery there comes to us a wonderful sense of freedom. Freedom from the compulsion to indulge ourselves, freedom from our past. Too many in our church are crippled and made miserable by yesterday's mistakes. They are ashamed and cannot forgive themselves; and the message from many a pulpit does not help. But the wonderful truth is that Jesus has set you free from all of that.

The next incident in Peter's life comes from the Mount of Transfiguration, recorded in Matthew 17. And again we see Peter a bit hasty and impetuous. He is ready to take charge before he really understands what is going on. He sees Moses and Elijah, and he thinks "Wow! This is great!" And he wants to build property. He wants to capture the moment and freeze it. There have always been some people who want to capture the sacred and keep it locked up so that the world does not contaminate it. They want to preserve spirituality on a health farm, or in a purer congregation, or in a more sacred formula.

But again revelation—the touch of God—breaks through, and Jesus says: "Let's go down from the mountain and meet the people." Peter had to learn that it is in the world among suffering, secular, ill-tempered, nasty, smelly, and at times very evil people that Christ's mission is to be finished; not in a reclusive formation on some "mountaintop."

That is where you can have a bit of adventure with Christ. And the Spirit will lead those who are prepared to walk with Christ to relate openly and positively to the world, and not out of fear and insecurity. Says Jesus: That is where the people are whom "God so much loved that He gave His only Son." So, He says, "Come out from your enclaves and meet the people!" And, "When you do, you will not be on your own." This is why the presence of the Holy Spirit is so often spoken of in terms of equipping the followers of Christ to be useful in His mission.

The next incident in Peter's life was that shocking experience when the disciples were in a boat and the sea was rough and stormy, and there they saw Jesus walking on the lake. Superstitious as most people are—and wouldn't you be if you had been there?—they cried out, "It's a ghost!"

"No," Jesus said, "it's Me! Remember?"

And again the focus is on the identity of Jesus. And we are again reminded of the fact that the constant and unchanging work of the Holy Spirit in our church and in our individual lives today, as well as in any "latter rain" experience, is to keep Christ in focus. And it is to help us understand who He is to you and me! For the invariable fact of life is that when Christ drifts out of focus and is replaced by other personal or corporate preoccupations, of which there are many, the waves come to swallow us up—and they do, as Peter discovered.

But there is this to be said for Peter: He wanted to go to the "refugee camp in Goma," he wanted to walk on the waves. He was certain that by doing so, although adventurous and dangerous as it might be, he would come closer to his Lord. And so he got out of the boat and began to walk. Do you think he ever forgot that experience? In our church there are people whose insistence on security is such that they venture nothing. They take no risks, and they are suspicious of anything that smells new or a bit adventurous. They will pray for those who go to a distant land as a volunteer, or to build a church, or to teach, or to feed a hungry child, but they wouldn't like to go there themselves.

Then there are those who when graduating from college say: "I want to experience some excitement with the Lord. I want to go to

Central Africa for a year and do something different; I want to go to Papua New Guinea or one of the other islands of the South Seas. I want to expand my education. I want to get to know the world in which the Lord has placed me." They are the wave-walkers who will step out because they feel within a deep desire for something more, something of greater value, something that will make a difference, something that will make me sleep better at night; yes, a bit of adventure with Christ. The song in their hearts is "Oh, for a closer walk with Thee," like the constant search between two lovers who seek and explore the limits of what each can give to the other. There is no room for "enough is enough." Because within us there is constant turning toward the Lord and a longing to feel His touch, His warmth, His understanding, His forgiveness, His encouragement, His assurance that He cares about us. We are unhappy with anything that creates a distance between the Lord and us. The Spirit is there to keep us close to the Lord.

The fourth incident is the fishing story recorded in John 21. As you will remember, they did not catch anything until Jesus came, and then the nets were full. John says that there were 153 fishes in the net. There was an ancient tradition that there were 153 known species of fish in the world. One of the early fathers, St. Jerome, tells us (and in a quaint sort of way thereby suggests that the mission of fishing, harvesting, or reaping that the church has to undertake is a universal one) that the mission is not finished until every kind of fish has been gathered in. And the net was not broken. The church is meant to have room for an amazing variety.

But this story is recorded after the events in John 20 where Jesus appeared before His disciples, and it says that He breathed on them and said, "Receive the Holy Spirit." The truth is that without the Spirit you cannot fish! The harvest is there, but without the power of the Spirit the reapers cannot work. The amazing fact, however, is that the Spirit is already there, but so many of the reapers do not know it. They behave as though they are in a state of waiting for the "golden future" of the Spirit instead of living up to the full potential of what is possible now, today!

Jesus said to Peter:

> Let me tell you something: When you were young you put on your own belt and walked where you liked; but when you grow old you will stretch out your hands and someone else will put a belt around you and take you where you would rather not go (see John 21:18).

That "someone else" is none other than the Spirit, and Peter was to discover just what that meant for him after Pentecost, culminating in his death.

In summary:

1. The Spirit leads us to identify Christ and to build our lives focused on Him, and allowing Him to bring His values into our lives.
2. He leads us down from whatever mountain we are on to mingle with people who have not yet discovered how deeply they are loved and how highly they are valued by God.
3. He invites us to be a bit adventurous in our lives of faith, away from just looking after ourselves and from being de-faulted to think and plan our own self-promotion. He invites us to discover that the best way to live life is to give of yourself for a cause or someone other than yourself.
4. He makes it possible for us to fish. Without Christ's presence the net is always empty, as is life, empty and barren.

The comforting words of Jesus to all of His followers who are prepared to look out, away from themselves, and take an interest in other people and give them hope, are " 'I will not leave you as orphans.' " " 'I am with you always' " (John 14:18; Mattthew 28:20).

CHAPTER FOUR

THE COMMUNITY OF THE SPIRIT

The prospect of Christ leaving His disciples after three-and-one-half years of friendship, fellowship, sharing of life, and instruction must have been cause for some concern among His immediate followers. What would become of them when He was gone? While genuine and sincere, they seemed so fickle and so unsure, so unpredictable and so ill-prepared to stand firmly for what they had come to know as Truth. They knew the truth, but would they be able to keep it in focus when He was gone? I remember the words of a University of Tubingen theologian about the resurrection of Jesus: "It happened so long ago that it is hardly true anymore." Can one survive as a believer when a long time passes between the promises and their fulfillment? Will it all stay sharp and in focus, or will it all seem a bit unreal?

Would the disciples survive and be true to Him on their own? Or is it possible that they would in fact never be on their own?

At various times Jesus tried to prepare them for the fact that He would be leaving (see, for example, Matthew 26:11; John 7:33, 34). Somehow they had to come to terms with that reality soon. The journeys they had made together would end. They would not continue to talk together and pray together as they had for three-and-one-half years. They would not see Him or touch Him anymore. He would be gone!

To prepare them for that potentially traumatic moment Jesus assured them that although He would physically leave them, He would never really leave them. " 'I am with you always, to the very end of the age' " (Matthew 28:20); " 'I will not leave you as orphans; I will come to you' " (John 14:18). God would take an initiative to maintain an unbroken continuity with the person and mission of Jesus Christ. Christ's ascension would not end God's literal and real presence among men. It would simply enter a new phase.

Fulfillment, as I have said before, was to come in the gift of the Holy Spirit, and He would continuously be present with the believers as long as God is engaged in the business of saving humanity. Pentecost marked the beginning of this new chapter.

Of course the Holy Spirit as the Third Person of the Godhead had been present and active among men since the beginning of time. However little the Jews of the Old Testament times had been able to conceive of God in Trinitarian terms (their belief was simply that "the Lord our God, the Lord is one" [Deuteronomy 6:4]), as one reads the Old Testament through the events of the New Testament one can see the Spirit was clearly there from the Creation moment onward. He was there inspiring the prophets (see 1 Kings 22:24; 2 Samuel 23:2; Isaiah 61:1; Ezekiel 11:5; Micah 3:8) and providing the gift of leadership to the judges (see Judges 3:10; 11:29). He was there as the One who creates out of nothing, whether we see Him in the Genesis Creation account or in the re-creation vision of Ezekiel 37. Mankind's natural origin is neither the dust of the earth nor bleached bones. It is God who creates, and He said to the prophet: " 'I will put my Spirit in you and you will live' " (Ezekiel 37:14).

Through His Spirit God has since the beginning of time been at work creating and recreating, designing and restoring. The community of God's people has always been the community of the Spirit. This is where He is and where He functions. "The Spirit recreates, refines, and sanctifies human beings, fitting them to become members of the royal family" (Ellen G. White, *Gospel Workers,* p. 287).

But when we come to the community of believers *after* the ascension of Christ, it is clear that a new "epoch of the Spirit" was to begin. He was to take on a set of functions among the believers and in the community that had not been seen before, at least not quite in that manner. Jesus, on whom the Holy Spirit was present without measure, taught His followers that after His own death and ascension something special would happen. The Spirit would come to the community of believers in a way they had not previously been accustomed to and in a role He had not had before. He would have a role and an assignment that would be particularly linked to the person and message of Jesus Christ. Therefore, this could begin only after Christ's ascension. The Spirit would then display His presence in a variety of gifts and functions. These gifts and functions were designed to help the community of believers remember and understand the teachings of Jesus; to equip them to live lives of discipleship and to witness to those who did not know Jesus Christ and had not accepted Him as Lord and Savior. In Jesus' parting message to His disciples as recorded in John chapters 14-16 He tells them about the coming of the Spirit and what the Spirit would do.

One of the difficulties the community of God's children faces after the ascension of Jesus Christ is that with the passing of time the messages of Jesus may not seem as sharp and clear as they once were. This may not be so much a matter of apostasy as it is the human frailty of *a dimmed vision and failing memory.* Each generation of believers lives in expectation of and with a deep longing for the return of the Lord, as He promised. But they will at times be perplexed by the apparent delay. So much time seems to pass. Is there something else that must happen before the Lord can return? Events will happen in history and on the secular scene that the believers will search the Scriptures to find meaning for. The believing mind turns to the prophetic and apocalyptic messages of the Bible to discover whether other events are foretold by inspired writers, which to the believers will be signposts or milestones on the journey to the Promised Land. How can the believer be sure that the interpretations arrived at are reliable and safe? The presence of the Holy Spirit makes it possible. He is the only safe Guide.

Furthermore, contemporary culture is constantly inviting all to reflect the culture in which they find themselves both in terms of values and lifestyle. And yet, believers know that God has already laid down the values that apply and the quality of life that the Christian is to espouse and follow. How can God's children be sure that they do not come adrift in these matters? How can they know that they take their directions from God and not from contemporary culture?

Again, the presence of the Holy Spirit is the answer. He is given to serve the needs of the church in these matters. He is present among the believers to guide, remind, and teach them.

"By His [the Holy Spirit's] power the vital truths upon which the salvation of the soul depends are impressed upon the mind, and the way of life is made so plain that none need err therein" (Ellen G. White, *Christ's Object Lessons,* p. 113). He is also the enabling Force who practically equips God's people to function as believers. "When by the Holy Spirit divine truths are impressed upon the heart, new conceptions are awakened, and the energies hitherto dormant are aroused to co-operate with God" (Ellen G. White, *The Acts of the Apostles,* p. 520).

The continuity between Jesus Christ in person and the Holy Spirit is clear. It is as though Christ is saying: "I told you then [when I was physically present among you], and I am telling you now [by the presence of the Spirit]."

Jesus made a solemn promise that a new epoch of the Spirit would soon come. The Father was committed to making a special endowment of the Spirit to the believers. Jesus said one day to His disciples: " 'If you then, though you are evil, know how to give good gifts to your children, how much more will your Father in heaven give the Holy Spirit to those who ask him!' " (Luke 11:13). Jesus on inviting those who were thirsty to come to Him and drink quoted Isaiah 58:11: " 'The Lord will guide you always; he will satisfy your needs. . . . You will be like a well-watered garden, like a spring whose waters never fail.' " Then the text reads: "By this he meant the Spirit, whom those who believed in him were later to receive. Up to that time the Spirit had not been given, since Jesus had not yet been glorified" (John 7:37-39). Clearly something of greatest importance for the spiritual welfare and effectiveness of the community of believers was about to happen. The thought of a special coming of the Spirit marks that beginning.

The gift of the Holy Spirit makes the difference! If the Spirit were not present among us today we would have no message to bring. We could relate some stories and tell of some interesting events, yes, but the sum of these, on their own, would not make up the gospel, and salvation would not come from them.

The role of the Holy Spirit is closely linked to the person and mission of Jesus Christ. The gift of the Holy Spirit is to make otherwise frail human beings into a genuine community of disciples of Christ. The spiritual gifts are to equip that community to function for Christ. Whilst the various gifts of the Spirit are given as God deems necessary and by His choice, the primary *gift* of the Holy Spirit is given to all who are genuinely committed to Jesus Christ and to living a life of obedience to Him. Paul, writing to a church that was greatly divided over spiritual gifts, made the point that all who have accepted Jesus Christ as their personal Savior and have by baptism been brought into the "body of Christ," which is the church, have this in common: that the one Holy Spirit has been poured out for them to drink (see 1 Corinthians 12:13). They have "tasted the heavenly gift" and "have shared in the Holy Spirit" (Hebrews 6:4).

One can well understand that some will find this difficult to grasp and accept. We may have been brought up to think that the gift of the Spirit belongs to an advanced, maybe more successful stage of our Christian journey, when the mistakes, with which our individual lives are sprinkled, are finished. Well, maybe not entirely, but at least we live better lives. We don't make the mistakes we once used to. And growth of this kind is normal; one would expect it to happen. It is a growth in the Spirit and a growth in Christ, and it is right. It must happen. And, yet, there is another clear reality. Sinfulness does not readily give up its cohabitation in the same body which now belongs to Christ and to which the Spirit has come as a gift. We are, as believers, covered by the righteousness of Christ while at the same time the presence of sin manifests itself in our lives. This tension is a reality we all live with and struggle with, and cannot deny! That is the way our humanity is. However, that does not mean the Holy Spirit is a stranger to us. The wonderful news is that it is possible to grow in the Spirit; it is possible to leave behind life patterns and mistakes of the past, but throughout this growing, life-changing development we belong to Christ. We are covered by His righteousness. The fact is that were it not for the presence of the Spirit in our lives we would not recognize the mistakes of the past as flaws in need of forgiveness and repair.

Paul is emphatic: It is not possible to be a believer—a follower of Christ—without the presence of the Spirit (Romans 8:9). Another important point that Paul makes (see Romans 8:16) is: "The Spirit testifies with our spirit that we are God's children." He is there to make us sure. I am meant to be able to say, not just that I hope I am a child of God, but that I *know* I am.

The outpouring of the Holy Spirit on the community of believers, as well as the manifestation of various gifts of the Spirit, are all "given for the common good" (1 Corinthians 12:7). Practically, what does that mean to us today?

1. Spiritual gifts are practical; they are for the good of the people. They are not meant as a private endowment given to an individual isolated from the community. Rather, it is all about the ability to function as a member of a larger body to whom a mission has been given. To live a spiritual life is therefore a very practical matter. And only those who are prepared to engage themselves practically can discover the reality of what it means to live by the Spirit. Being a Christian is best defined in what one does for others (see Ephesians

4:12). And, therefore, everyone must ask, What am I doing? What occupies the days of my week? What do I call important? Does the quality of life of other people become better because I am there? Or is it possible that my presence has no practical consequence in the lives of other people? The Holy Spirit's presence is meant to be a catalyst for change.

2. The Gift of the Spirit is linked to " 'power from on high' " (Luke 24:49). Spirit-filled-ness is the opposite of weakness, lethargy, and confusion. It has to do with power to be and to act, and it lifts us to a level where we otherwise would not be. And this power is nothing other than the power of creation. It is the power to take what *is not* and make something of wonder and beauty out of it. And as we look at ourselves, do we not find cause to be thankful for the fact that God creates out of nothing? When all is said and done, what do we have to offer except a willing heart that has been surrendered to Jesus Christ? That very same reality was what Pentecost signified. The Creator-Spirit took a group of uncertain, frightened, and discouraged individuals and made them into witnesses who go forth with unstoppable conviction and motivation. It was the Spirit who did it—and who does it today.

3. The Spirit was given to make one people, one family, out of many individuals, united in peace (see Ephesians 4:3), without division (1 Corinthians 1:10), and loving one another. When that happens the climate in the church becomes such that individuals want to belong and make it their home. The church is meant to offer a "consumer-friendly" environment, even to those whose battle scars are visible.

It is no coincidence that the fruits of the Spirit find their meaning only in relationships with other people (see Galatians 5:22; Ephesians 4:32). It is also no coincidence that the chapter on love (1 Corinthians 13) is placed in the midst of Paul's treatment of spiritual gifts. The unity in the church is organic; life and nurture is to flow from one individual to the next. That is the meaning of being one "Body." It is the Spirit that binds us together.

And here I must pause and ask myself: What is it that comes from me and is shared with my brothers and sisters in the church? Is it something that gives life, hope, encouragement, a reason to go on; or is it discouraging, negative, critical, cynical, and ultimately destructive of life itself?

Spirituality is always a very practical matter, and it has practical consequences always. So it is for us today. Instead of living in the hope that one day the Spirit will come also to me, I can live today fully as the Spirit who is with me makes it possible now. Instead of living with just a dream and hope—which we also do—we learn to live with some spiritual realities which are here now. Out of that comes a strong and attractive Christian life.

"For as many as are led by the Spirit of God, these are sons of God . . . and if children, then heirs—heirs of God and joint heirs with Christ, if indeed we suffer with Him, that we may also be glorified together" (Romans 8:14, 17, NKJV). Give yourself a chance to experience the richness and fullness of the life of the Spirit—NOW!

CHAPTER FIVE

BEING
USEFUL
TO GOD

Isaiah 6:1-8

Isaiah the prophet was born into the royal family, so it is thought. He lived in the eighth century B.C. This was a difficult time in Israel's history. Internally, the people's morale was sagging. The country was plagued with injustice, immorality, abuse of the poor, and idolatry. Externally, the Northern Kingdom was about to be overrun by the Assyrian forces. But even in such a time of national crisis the people, and not least their leaders, indulged in their waywardness and apostasy. Decadence, like a cancer, was eating away at the health of the society.

The kings of both the Northern and the Southern Kingdoms were on the whole a pretty poor lot, largely unable to give the kind of leadership God wanted for His people. They were as spiritually and morally bankrupt as were the people for whom they were leaders. The future seemed bleak and hopeless. And what happened over the next two centuries, culminating in the Babylonian captivity, must be seen against the background of the internal decay of God's people.

In Isaiah 6, however, we meet one of the better kings: Uzziah. He had ruled for more than fifty years, and it is very probable that Isaiah knew him well. He may have even grown up at the court of the king. But, alas, Uzziah also became a marked man during the latter years of his life. He had not respected what God had called holy, and the Lord struck him with leprosy as punishment for his failure to respect what God had said. If your leaders, in a community and among a people supposed to be led by God, will not let God and His standards guide them, then things will go from bad to worse, and before you know it you are hovering on the brink of disaster. God needed at least some leaders who could lift the vision and the hearts of the people to better things. But, sadly, in this also Uzziah failed.

God expected then, as He does now, that His chosen leaders have the will and the vision to lead the people on a safe course to better ways and a better life, even though the leaders also belong to fallen humanity, and they have their frailty, their shortcomings, and their history. They also need to ask God daily for forgiveness for their failures, and they, too, cry out for help, as I do. Yet God also sustains His leaders if they have the will and humility to listen to Him and be led by the Spirit of God. God never calls and then abandons His chosen ones. That has never been God's pattern. Our commitment is often fickle; God's is not.

Uzziah was not the best king, but there had been many leaders who were a lot worse. It is quite probable that Isaiah was fond of the old king. With half a century as the ruler he was a known quantity and he represented stability. And when he died, Isaiah probably felt the pains of grief and loss. And he may have wondered: What now? What is going to happen? Whom do we now have to lead us? We are faced with weakness, corruption, and decay among the people; and from outside there are the threatening dangers. Who is there to lead us into the uncertain future?

It was in those circumstances and at that moment of distress that God spoke to Isaiah. And the circumstances are important to note. "In the year that King Uzziah died, I saw the Lord," says the text. And God will do that sort of thing sometimes. We all go through moments in life when we feel troubled and uncertain and insecure about the future, and the nagging pain is eating away at us. We are troubled about ourselves—about things we would like to change but we don't know how. We are troubled about our families; troubled by illnesses and pains that we find difficult to carry; troubled by uncertainties and loneliness, death in the family, a divorce. We don't know how to cope with the waywardness of a child, failure of a crucial exam, loss of a job, losses on the stock market, anger with a husband because he accepted a new position which means that we have to uproot and move yet again. There are moments in the lives of all of us that for one reason or other throw our lives into disarray. And we begin to wonder and reflect; we probe and search for reasons or signals. We ask: "God, are You there? Can You hear me? What have You got to say? Just a word—just a word!" These are moments when we are particularly sensitive to any signal God might be sending our way.

And so it was with Isaiah. He says that in the year when death struck an important person in his family, "I saw the Lord."

And just what did he see? Does he see the Lord Almighty in a state of agitation or disarray, walking anxiously and restlessly back and forth in the heavenly corridors wondering how He can best restore decency among His people and deal with the threatening enemy to the northeast? Does he see a God who is frustrated with the bureaucratic processes of slow-working committees? Does he see a God who is anxiously examining and reflecting over the latest financial statement? This is not a God worried about bin Laden or other reactionary fundamentalists. This is not a God troubled by Wall Street.

No. This God is sitting down majestically, quietly, and serenely. He is the Sovereign God, supremely in charge of planets, kingdoms, events, and circumstances; a God who is never surprised, never caught off-guard, and never unprepared. He sits there high and exalted in His throne room, from which the activities of the universe are governed. Our God is the Almighty God! He has the full view of everything that "was, is, and shall be." There are no surprises to Him!

And around the throne was a choir of angels (seraphim), multiple-winged creatures. They formed an antiphonal choir, and as they spread out in opposite rows on each side of the throne of God, one group sang out and the other answered:

> "Holy, holy, holy is the Lord Almighty;
> the whole earth is full of his glory" (Isaiah 6:3).

They sang it over and over and over again, and the sound of their voices was such that the very doorposts and thresholds shook, the very foundations came alive. As Isaiah beholds this he is overawed by a sense of the purity, the holiness, the majesty, and the sovereignty of God. It is more than he can take in! And he cannot cope with it, because at that same moment he becomes acutely aware of himself, and he is totally flummoxed. His flawed smallness and God's immeasurable greatness! The contrast is more than he can take, and he cries out:

"Woe to me! . . . I am ruined! For I am a man of unclean lips, and I live among a people of unclean lips, and my eyes have seen the King, the Lord Almighty" (verse 5).

It is clear that this whole scene is more than Isaiah can cope with. He is overwhelmed, he is frightened, he is broken, and he feels distinctly out of place. He sees the Sovereign God, he hears the unmatched heavenly choir, and he hears God's infinite holiness being affirmed by the universe. And then, just as he is doing that, he becomes aware of himself. What a letdown!

Two sentences belong together here, as the left hand and the right:

1. "Holy, holy, holy is the Lord Almighty"; and

2. "Woe to me! . . . I am ruined! For I am a man of unclean lips."

They belong together in the framework of a believing, worshiping mind that senses the greatness of God, accompanied by a correspondingly modest view of oneself. Later we shall notice that God very specifically gives Isaiah a call. Isaiah becomes a man chosen by God. He fits into God's design. God has plans for him. But before Isaiah can begin to function in the role God has for him, God shows Himself to Isaiah. God does not begin preparing Isaiah for the task ahead by showing to Isaiah the size of the challenge before him, particularly the oppression of the poor, the injustices, and idolatry that were so rampant. No, He begins by leading Isaiah to a one-to-one encounter with Himself. It is as though He says to Isaiah: "Isaiah, I want you to have a good look at Me. Isaiah, look this way! Isaiah, I want you to know Me. Look at Me. This is what I am like. And, Isaiah, you cannot become and do what I have in mind for you unless and until you have seen Me."

And seeing God is the thing that blew Isaiah away.

You do not have to be particularly gifted or have a special education to be useful to God. But you have to be honest, and you have to be willing to listen to what God says; and you have to recognize your limitations.

It is, of course, conceivable that God could have done this differently. He could have shown Isaiah the challenge before him. He could have shown him how seriously and how far the people of Israel had come adrift from the Lord and His plans. And could have appealed to the noblest of qualities and honorable sentiments in Isaiah, and tried to convince Isaiah that he was the ideal man for the job. That is the way we often do it when we select someone for a particular assignment. But that is not the way God did it this time. He wanted to be sure that Isaiah had seen God. Before any other consideration entered the picture it was important that Isaiah had seen the Almighty, because only in that context can you truly see yourself.

Isaiah said of himself that he was a man of "unclean lips." I don't know just what that meant, but I notice that when the angel came with a coal from the altar to cleanse Isaiah, it was his lips that he touched. Maybe Isaiah was given to easy use of foul language. Who knows? But what matters is that God dealt with it. And this is the wonder and beauty of it all: God can deal with whatever shortcoming it may be. God will not accept our excuses for noninvolvement.

There was another man—the most famous man in Israel's history—who, when God called him, began to think of excuses. Moses said to God, "You have got this one wrong. Who am I to go to Egypt?"

God said: "I will go with you."

"Well," said Moses, "suppose I go and they begin to ask me difficult questions, such as 'Who sent you?' What do I say?"

God told him what to say. "And what if they don't believe me?"

God said, "They will."

Moses said: "I am not good at speaking; I never have been. Sending me is not a good idea. I have a better idea."

The text says that God got quite exasperated with Moses (see Exodus 4:14) and He said: "Look, I know you are tongue-tied. Your brother, Aaron, is a better speaker, and he is already on his way to go with you."

There is no end to the list of reasons we put before God as we look for a way out, justifying our noninvolvement. Haven't we all done that?

"Lord, I am not the one You are looking for."

"I don't have the talents required."

"I need some more education."

"Lord, I just got married."

"I cannot manage on the salary they're paying; I would have to change my lifestyle."

"Lord, this is a bad time to sell property and I've just bought this house."

"Lord, I don't think my wife is going to like this, and my mother-in-law will get all steamed up."

"Lord, I know just the right person for this task."

And the list is endless. We are good at tailor-making our excuses to fit our personal situation.

But when God speaks to us He tells us that He is bigger than any of the excuses we have to offer for noninvolvement. And God is particularly good at taking bruised, broken, soiled, and rejected "vessels" and making them whole, forgiven, and useful again. In the words of the song:

"All I had to offer Him was brokenness and strife
But He made something beautiful of my life."

That is the heart of the gospel, the wonder of it all. Remember what the angel said to Isaiah: "Your iniquity is removed, and your sin is wiped away" (6:7, NEB).

What a wonderful affirmation! Where sin abounds, grace super-abounds! (See Romans 5:20.)

The one thing Isaiah was unable to deal with and conquer God dealt with. That is the way God is. He gives us hope, and He helps us to know that whatever we may contain, whatever may be stored in our closets, whatever history there may have been, God can deal with it and resolve it. And we can become useful for God. There is before God no acceptable reason for noninvolvement. Discipleship is not a spectator sport!

But listen to the dialogue as it develops between Isaiah and God:

> Then I heard the voice of the Lord saying,
> "Whom shall I send? And who will go for us?"
> And I said, "Here am I. Send me!"
> He said, "Go and tell this people . . ." (6:8).

Remember the sequence in which this happened:

- After Isaiah has seen the Lord in His full majesty and awesome beauty, worshiped by the unfallen universe;
- After Isaiah had then seen himself and acknowledged his shortcomings, and had had the courage and honesty to admit them to himself and to God;
- After God had assured Isaiah that He could take care of Isaiah's shortcomings, that He had forgiven his failings; that in spite of knowing full well his flaws, He said that He wanted him and He gave him a feeling of value and being useful.

Then He said: "Will you go for Me, Isaiah? Are you

willing to be shaped and molded and used by Me in My mission?"

And that is the question God puts to each of us!

Isaiah's testimony is simply this: Against the background of what I have just experienced and what I have just seen, how could I say anything but "Yes, I will go"?

In order to achieve His mission, God deals effectively with limitations and shortcomings that we struggle with. We know our flaws, and we talk with God about them. They are acknowledged and they are then resolved. As God exposed to Isaiah, so He exposes to you and me a world and a mission such as we have never seen or understood before. And one becomes strangely moved and motivated to break loose from the tight little circle that most of us have erected around ourselves—a circle of *my* career, *my* plans, *my* future, *my* social life; and one becomes strangely aware of another world—God's world, God's future, and God's plans.

And then even more strangely, God tells Isaiah a little about the success, or lack of it, he will have on his mission. God says, "When you communicate with the people on My behalf, you will sadly discover that when you talk they will be hearing and hearing, but never really hearing you; they will be seeing but never really see; their hearts are callused, their eyes are shut, and their ears are dull" (see 6:9, 10).

A pretty hopeless picture! The response you get from the people will suggest that it is all quite hopeless.

Then Isaiah says to the Lord, "How long are You going to put up with this?" (see 6:11).

And God says to Isaiah: "Don't get yourself frustrated by that, and don't think it is all in vain because you do not see the early fruits. I have My own schedule and My own scale for measuring success. Rest assured, it will not be in vain. When everything looks fruitless and barren, there is a *remnant;* there is a 'holy seed' left in the stump in the land" (see verse 13).

It does us good when we can see that what we are doing is succeeding. We thrive on awareness that it is not wasted effort. We are all human beings, and it gives us all a lift to see the fruit of our labor. But in God's work that is not always easy to sustain. So I say to you: *The greatest affirmation that we need is not the tangible, statistically measurable results of our efforts, but the inner assurance and knowledge that we are partners with God in His mission and His plans.* For then you know also that you have a place in God's future. And the only thing you can take with you out of this life is the future!

So what do you say? Does it appeal to you?

Said Paul: "If I am sharing the gospel of salvation with someone, I can claim no credit for it; I am simply discharging the trust committed to me" (see 1 Corinthians 9:17).

We are not studying these things just for the sake of understanding a passage of Scripture. This is all done for the further purpose of our making decisions. God expects each of us to make decisions. It is God who appeals to you and me and He says: "You are useful to Me. Can I count on you? Will you come?

"You say you have flaws and you carry baggage?" God asks. "I know them better than you know them yourself. But I can forgive, and I can heal, and I can make you strong. Let Me make you useful to Me."

And ahead lie a wonderful life and a fascinating journey with the Lord.

NOT VERY FAIR!

Matthew 20:1-16

So much of what Jesus had to say and teach came in the form of stories. Some came in the imagery of something that had really happened, others were imagined happenings. It did not really matter which as long as it served to illustrate something He wanted to say. This was His favored teaching method, and so the Bible says of Jesus that He spoke to the people "in parables, at some length" (Matthew 13:3, NEB). Even the disciples asked: " 'Why do you speak to them in parables?' " (Matthew 13:10, NEB).

And the reasons were several.

Jesus was not a theoretician; He was not given to systematic presentations of technical points. So much of what Jesus said, and that is particularly true of the many stories He told, were uttered on the edge of some confrontation. The parables did not lay down general maxims; they were verbal weapons used at moments of tension and controversy. And the tensions were often between the religious leaders and the common people, or between the views of the Pharisees and Jesus.

From the point of view of the religious leaders of the day Jesus of Nazareth was a difficult person to have around; He was provocative and, in their view, not a good influence on the simple people. And here we meet immediately one of the great paradoxes of Jesus: He was the Creator of genuine spirituality, the Father of the religious culture of Israel, and yet He was One in whose presence the leaders of religion felt insecure and threatened. And in contrast, those who were inclined to feel attracted to Jesus were precisely those whom the religious structure of the day had made to feel as outcasts.

There was a lot of tension caused by religion—there often is. God was projected as harsh and vindictive, and finding anything that could be called surety of salvation was complicated and difficult to obtain.

This was the scene upon which Jesus stepped and spoke in parables "at some length." The stories gave Him the opportunity to be gone and minister elsewhere while the religious leaders tried to figure out what He had actually said. And the themes Jesus kept coming back to in His stories were questions that the ordinary people had about God:

- How does God look upon and treat people?
- How does God expect us to relate to people?
- What is God like?
- What is His kingdom like? How do I gain entrance to it?
- Why does God not like us? It is hard enough to be poor and ill, but why should God also be against us?

It must be hard to be God when the very persons whom God has entrusted with spiritual leadership give a distorted impression of God and they make Him look like a vindictive and harsh ruler. As a minister I have the responsibility to help and not hinder a meeting between God and sinners. I am there to teach the truth about God and the love of God, and not to obstruct it.

In Matthew 19 a story is told in the setting of a conversation Jesus had just had with a rich young man who went away, it says, with "a heavy heart" when he discovered what a radical choice discipleship is. Jesus had made it clear to the young ruler that discipleship is a life of obedience. And the young man thought that that was precisely what he had excelled at. But he had an inner fear that all was not well; and he asked: "What do I still lack?" What happened next revealed his love for his wealth. That particular incident led Jesus to make the famous statement that " 'it is easier for a camel to go through the eye of a needle than for a rich man to enter the kingdom of God' " (Matthew 19:24), an assertion that was absolutely astounding when you consider the widely held notion that if a man was rich he was so because God looked with favor upon him!

All of this is most confusing to Peter, who counters: "Then what about us? ' "We have left everything to follow you! What then will there be for us?" ' " (verse 27). I find it heartwarming that Jesus does not rebuke Peter for his somewhat mercenary approach to discipleship. Peter needed time to grow and mature in his fellowship with the Lord, as is true for us all, and the Lord allows him (and us) time and space for that to happen. But Jesus assures Peter that discipleship will not go unrewarded; even so He adds a warning: " 'Many who are first will be last, and [the] last will be first' " (verse 30), by which He introduces the story in Matthew 20:

A landowner went out early one morning at 6:00 to hire workers for his vineyard. He found some and agreed with them the standard day's wages, one dinar. Then he went out at 9:00 in the morning and hired some more workers and agreed that they also would be paid a "fair wage." Similarly at noon he went out, and then again at 3:00 he went out and hired some more. Even at 5:00 P.M. he hired some more workers for his vineyard. At 6:00 P.M. he called them all together for the pay. To the annoyance of some, but the delight of others, but no doubt to everyone's surprise, he paid them all the same: one dinar.

So, what is Jesus trying to say with this story?

Everything that we may say about the meaning of this story must be seen against the background that God is in the business of giving hope to people who for one reason or other have been made to feel unwanted or rejected by God; and when it comes to the gift of salvation, God is wonderfully generous. So, the story is about how God treats people. It says something about what God is like.

First, it reminds us that even in the last hour there are people milling about—just killing time—because "no one has hired us." They are available, they are receptive, they are open and looking for maybe they know not what, but they are looking. And unless they are being approached and spoken to—and that means somebody has to come physically near them and speak to them—the day of opportunity will have passed and God's invitation will have not reached them.

This is a very serious matter for us as a missionary movement focused on the growth of the community of believers. *God never gives up on people; neither must we.*

We may look at selected church growth statistics and conclude that God is "elsewhere"; nothing is happening where I live, and the Spirit has moved off to Africa, or Latin America, or some spots in Asia. That is not the case. God's commitment to people everywhere is unrelenting. And He is asking us not to quit or write people off. We may say, "Oh, they would not be interested" (about our neighbors). How do you know? When did you last talk with them about God and the future?

The wage paid at the end of the day shows that God does not reward on the *quid pro quo* principle. It was quite remarkable that the landowner should pay them all the same. The fact is that you could not survive on anything less. *There is no surplus in it;* it is what you need in order to live, in order to have a future. It is all about salvation, and in the Bible there is no such idea as "salvation plus." Being secure for eternity is enough.

But it is also clear that the reward or the gift is in no way related to the effort or contribution of those who accepted the invitation. But the gift says everything about God. It is out of kindness, compassion, love, and pity that the Master gives those who come at the last hour the same as those who have stayed the full course. This is the thought Paul captures when he says, "Not for any good deeds of our own, but because he was merciful, he saved us" (Titus 3:5, NEB). David beautifully captured the same thought in one of his psalms:

> The Lord is compassionate and gracious, slow to
> anger, abounding in love. . . .
> He does not treat us as our sins deserve. . . .
> For as high as the heavens are above the earth,
> so great is his love for those who fear him. . . .
> As a father has compassion on his children,
> so the Lord has compassion on those who fear him
> (Psalm 103:8-13).

But the wages at the end of the day do say something about the laborers: They accepted the invitation and came. No "gift" would have come their way had they just wished the landowner good luck with his harvest and then drifted their own way.

The next thought from the story is illustrated by the reaction of those who had worked all day. Now, we may think that their reaction was not very charitable, but I wonder whether most of us do not feel a bit of sympathy for them. After all, they had sweated a whole day and worked hard. Somehow I wonder whether most of us quite instantaneously would not feel that an offense was committed against natural justice. Surely it is offensive to any notion of "equal pay for equal work," and they had not all worked equally. Some felt they had been treated unjustly. But they had not. The landowner kept his word and paid them what they had agreed. But other sentiments began to take over—sentiments of jealousy and greed—which give birth to negative and destructive feelings toward others.

All that the landowner had done was to show kindness and generosity to those who by their efforts clearly could make no claim to have earned their "wage." And Jesus said: " ' "Why be jealous because I am kind?" ' " (verse 15, NEB). Salvation is a gift from the heart of God. It is given because He is generous. It has nothing to do with anything "earned" or *quid pro quo,* but it has everything to do with accepting the invitation.

The Pharisees felt very uncomfortable with this story and the lessons it hinted at. They just did not understand, as indeed I also so often tend to overlook, that God is ever on the lookout for people who, were it not for the totally undeserved kindness of God, would be hopelessly lost. Jesus is on the lookout for losers. That's the way God is; and as His minister I must take care so as not to obscure or distort this important truth about God.

Jesus turned to one of those who had worked twelve hours and who somehow could not take in good grace the obviously undeserved kindness that some were receiving, and who had expressed his anger or frustration to the landowner, feeling that he should have been granted some preference above the latecomers, and said to him: " ' "Friend, I am not being unfair to you" ' " (verse 13).

And even in this, another aspect of God's generosity is seen. It does me good to know that on occasions a person may display a temperament or personality trait that is alien or unacceptable to God and still be called "friend." Three times in the Gospels we find Jesus using the expression "friend," and every time it is to persons who are obviously in the wrong (e.g., to the man who got in to the wedding feast without his wedding garment on [Matthew 22:12]; and to Judas the traitor in the Garden [Matthew 26:50]).

Who are these persons who have put in a full twelve-hour day and who feel that they deserve something more—maybe a special recognition? They are persons who for one reason or another have come to feel that they are ahead of the rest. "They think more of the reward than of the privilege of being servants of Christ" (Ellen G. White, *Christ's Object Lessons*, p. 400). And they think, *Surely God will find a way of recognizing and acknowledging that I—we— deserve something extra. After all, we have done so much!*

> The Jews had first been called into the Lord's vineyard and because of this they were proud and self-righteous. . . . Nothing was more exasperating to them than an intimation that the Gentiles were to be admitted to equal privileges with themselves in the things of God" (Ibid).

Self-righteousness is a potential curse of the church even today!

As one ponders the depth of meaning contained in this story told by Jesus, the two main thoughts, among many, that linger are:

1. "Let not the wise man boast of his wisdom or the strong man boast of his strength or the rich man boast of his riches, but let him who boasts boast about this: that he understands and knows me, that I am the Lord, who exercises kindness, justice and righteousness on earth, for in these I delight," declares the Lord (Jeremiah 9:23, 24). The reward is all of grace.

2. To accept the Lord's invitation, to go with Him and to serve Him, is a privilege which at the end of the day is not rewarded with a well-earned remuneration, but with an undeserved gift; a gift which does not describe my efforts, but is a characteristic of the loving-kindness of our Lord. He is generous beyond measure. "No one is privileged above another, nor can anyone claim the reward as a right" (Ellen G. White, *Christ's Object Lessons*, p. 402).

The parable is a warning to all laborers, however long their service, however brilliant their record, however many terms of elected office they have held, however many years they have served in overseas mission, that without love to their colleagues, and without humility before God, they are nothing. The smallest duty done in sincerity and with sacrifice is more pleasing to God than the greatest deed marred by a spirit of self-seeking and self-promotion.

"Then one of the elders asked me: 'These in white robes—who are they and where did they come from?'

"I answered, 'Sir, you know.' And he said, 'These are they who have come out of the great tribulation; they have washed their robes and made them white in the blood of the Lamb. . . .

"For the Lamb at center of the throne will be their shepherd; he will lead them to springs of living water. And God will wipe away every tear from their eyes' " (Revelation 7:13-17).

Amen. Come, Lord Jesus!

CHAPTER SEVEN

THE
JOURNEY

Hebrews 11:8-10

Down through the ages God's people have always seen themselves as a people on the move. There is a certain nomadic quality to the Christian life, not in the sense of moving without a goal or drifting from one pasture to another, but in the sense that "where I am today is not where I shall always be." This is not my permanent home; something hinted at by Jesus when He said that His followers may be "in the world" but they are not "of it." God's people are pilgrims, and His call to them has always been, " 'Come out of her, my people' " (Revelation 18:4). "Come, walk with Me. I will take you to a better place. I have something richer, something more secure and permanent for you. Walk with Me and I will take you there," says God.

The mentality of a pilgrim is well illustrated by Abraham. His epitaph reads:

> By faith he obeyed and accepted God's invitation to become a pilgrim;
>
> By faith he chose to live as a "stranger in a foreign country," and he did not see himself as belonging to that environment; he was a traveler—he was just passing through; and
>
> By faith he was destined for the city "whose architect and builder is God."

A pilgrim is ever conscious of the destination—it may be in the distance, but it is never out of focus. An indescribable longing for that future fills you and draws you toward that destiny. A pilgrim becomes bold and uninhibited when he or she confesses: "I don't belong here. I am on my way to the future that God has designed for me. If I had wanted to go back to where I came from, I could have done so, but I am finished with that, I have made my choice, and I am on my way to something better."

And in harmony with that, you and I, who have made our choice and have stepped out, we choose our values and our lifestyles.

It strikes me that when Abraham, as the proto-pilgrim, is described (see Hebrews 11:8-10), the words *faith* and *obedience* are prominent. The fact is that faith has no other way of expressing itself than by obedience. Anyone whose understanding labors with a tension between faith and obedience is already off on a bad start. The very acceptance of salvation in Jesus Christ is itself an act of obedience to the Lord, and from there on the mode of the mind and heart of the believer is constantly searching for the will of the Lord. Faith does not pause to ensure or protect itself against all the unknowns of tomorrow. It was clear to Abraham, as it is to all of his spiritual children, that he was on a journey, and that God's destiny is better than anything you encounter on the way. And out of this come some eternal truths that we need to identify and hold on to.

1. It is a fact of life—it certainly was so in the ancient world, but we see it also today among refugees—that strangers or refugees are viewed with a certain distance, a certain uneasiness, a certain suspicion and also often with contempt.

An ancient "Letter of Aristeas" states: "It is a fine thing to live and die in one's native land; (in) a foreign land . . . there is the lurking suspicion that they have been exiled for the evil they have done" (Barclay, *Letter to the Hebrews,* p. 168). Somehow they were not trusted to be constructive members of the society in which they lived. They didn't belong. "Why don't they go back to where they came from?"

There was in the ancient world an unwritten saying attributed to Jesus: "The world is a bridge. The wise man will pass over it but will not build his house upon it" (Ibid.). The early Christian Fathers returned often in their writings to the theme that believers are sojourners, their destiny is in God's future; and that is where they belong. This, however, did not make them hostile to or disinterested in the society in which they found themselves, but the sense of belonging to eternity was the overwhelmingly dominant identity of a pilgrim; and that is how they saw themselves.

2. A pilgrim never loses faith in the future. The journey is never too long, and the attraction to giving up is never valid. Short cuts and compromises were viewed as distractions and unacceptable. As Enoch walked with God, so a pilgrim is ever conscious of the fact that he or she is never alone; that God is a constant Companion.

To memory comes an incident from my childhood. Toward the end of the Second World War, Norway was still occupied, and food, where I lived, was not in abundance. One day a Lapp (one of a semi-nomadic people attending their flocks of reindeer), who lived in a small cabin in a secluded area some fifteen miles from my home, came to my father and asked if he could "borrow" me for two months of the summer to do some shepherding. He promised that he would feed me well. I was nine years old, growing, but could use more food. My father agreed.

This was summer in northern Norway, and the sun did not set, so we had daylight for twenty-four hours. One evening, having spent the day up in the hills with some of his animals, including some goats, and brought them down into a hedged-in area for the night, I went to sleep in the cabin. The Lapp woke me up after midnight and said: "Two of the goats are missing. You have to go up in the hills to find them."

As I made my way up the path into the hills I felt miserable, forgotten by my family, and I was convinced that no one cared for me. After all, I was just nine years old, I told myself. It was raining; and as the water ran down my face it had a salty taste to it as water mixed with tears. I was totally alone—forgotten by all!

Then I felt something touch my hand. It was my sheep-dog licking my fingers, telling me that I was not alone. I had forgotten about him while feeling so sorry for myself. And he sensed that. And he wanted me to know that he was with me. What a difference it made as we made our way up and found the goats.

Said the Lord: "I will never leave you, I will never forsake you."

The pilgrims of old lived in hope, and even when the hour came when they were laid to rest the expectations for God's future never weakened.

3. To turn around and go back to where you came from has no attraction to a pilgrim. Yes, there are days when the smells from the meat-pots of Egypt will tickle the nostrils, and for a fleeting moment the memories may be sweet, but that is all. Going back to where we have come from has no lasting attraction, because it has no future. A pilgrim has already "tasted the heavenly gift . . . the goodness of the word of God and the powers of the coming age" (Hebrews 6:4, 5), and going back now is the utmost folly. No, our course is set, and our intention is to keep it "steady as you go."

And yet to many a pilgrim there is an open sore inside because I know that there is someone whom I carry in my heart who is no longer traveling with me. What happened? Was "Egypt" really that appealing? Did the future become unreal and somehow too distant? Was I too busy with my own things to talk to my friend about hope, about promises, about joy, and about eternity?

The prayer in my heart that cries out is: "Forgive me, O Lord, for my failings. Lord, please, go back and look for my friend."

4. A pilgrim is someone whom God claims as His. It says of Enoch that he walked with God, and then he was no more because God took him to Himself (see Genesis 5:24). Very fundamentally a pilgrim *belongs* to God already, here, while journeying, and he *knows it;* and God is not "ashamed to be called their God" (Hebrews 11:16) because that affinity—that closeness—is already now a reality.

I am reminded of the beautiful and moving words of the Psalm that describe this closeness between God and the pilgrim on the journey to the kingdom:

I will lift up my eyes to the mountains;
From whence shall my help come?
My help comes from the Lord,
Who made heaven and earth.
He will not allow your foot to slip;
He who keeps you will not slumber.
Behold, He who keeps Israel
Will neither slumber nor sleep.

The Lord is your keeper;
The Lord is your shade on your right hand;
The sun will not smite you by day,
Nor the moon by night.
The Lord will protect you from all evil;
He will keep your soul.
The Lord will guard your going out and your coming in
From this time forth and forever (Psalm 121, NASB).

Both Abraham's journey out of Ur of the Chaldeans and Israel's Exodus from Egypt were events in history that became symbols of the journey of the believers through life. The believers readily confess that they are "aliens and strangers on earth" (Hebrews 11:13); or in the words of Paul: They would prefer to be "at home with the Lord" (2 Corinthians 5:8). The two: Exodus and the journey ahead belong together. Once you have taken the step, you are, in a sense, already "marked." You are on your way. Maybe wobbling a bit; maybe unsure of yourself; maybe ashamed of the baggage you carry; maybe ridiculed, or whatever. But you have stepped out and you have become a pilgrim, and you are on your way, and you belong to the Lord. And no one can take the inheritance away from you. Said our Lord: " 'You do not belong to the world, but I have chosen you out of the world' " (John 15:19). In talking to His Father about us Jesus said: " 'My prayer is not that you take them out of the world [a point that may be worth keeping in mind by those who may be overly attracted by the wilderness] but that you protect them from the evil one' " (John 17:15). Therefore, "Our citizenship is in heaven. And we eagerly await a Savior from there" (Philippians 3:20).

So, do not hesitate in showing your "color" and your values, and your "nationality"; and do not become distracted or discouraged. Discouragement is the devil's most effective instrument to destroy your pilgrimage. I am reminded of the inspired counsel as to how we should treat each other on the journey:

> You will often meet with souls that are under the stress of temptation. You know not how severely Satan may be wrestling with them. Beware lest you discourage such souls and thus give the tempter an advantage.
>
> Whenever you see or hear something that needs to be corrected, seek the Lord for wisdom and grace, that in trying to be faithful you may not be severe.
>
> It is always humiliating to have one's errors pointed out. Do not make the experience more bitter by needless censure. Unkind criticism brings discouragement, making life sunless and unhappy.
>
> My brethren, prevail by love rather than by severity. When one at fault becomes conscious of his error, be careful not to destroy his self-respect. Do not seek to bruise and wound, but rather to bind up and heal (Ellen G. White, *Testimonies for the Church*, 7:265).

Rather than being instruments of discouragement we owe it to each other to lighten the burden, and bring some hope into each other's life, and a sense of being wanted and feeling safe. We are in this together; we share a common destiny; and I am going to be your neighbor in eternity.

Peter, having stated that God's elect are "strangers in the world," says that we are going to have to learn to live our lives as strangers to the world and its values (see 1 Peter 1:1, 17; 2:11). But this is not projected as a heavy price to pay or as some kind of sacrifice. It is not as though we are giving up the "good life" and are left with something that is trimmed back to the bone, as it were, as some kind of minimum-quality life. The life of the believer is different because she or he is different. But it is a rich and happy and full life. It is different, but that is because it belongs to the Lord and to the future, and to a new world and to a new order.

Paul admonishes the pilgrim to get dressed for the journey; put on (see Ephesians 6):

1. The belt of truth; yes, true doctrines, but I believe also being truthful and honest;

2. The breastplate of righteousness—the protection that comes from knowing we are covered by Christ;

3. Shoes that will keep us agile and enable us to scale the "mountains," bringing good news and proclaiming peace (Isaiah 52:7);

4. The shield of faith by which we deflect the attacks of the evil one—in fact without which you would be too vulnerable—that keeps the community of faith together. Alone we are exposed; together we are strong. To my mind come the words familiar to every Adventist: "Press together. Press together." God said to Abraham: " 'Do not be afraid. I am your shield' " (Genesis 15:1).

5. The helmet of salvation by which we are assured that "we are more than conquerors through him who loved

us. For I am convinced that neither death nor life, neither angels nor demons, neither the present nor the future, nor any powers . . . will be able to separate us from the love of God that is in Christ Jesus our Lord" (Romans 8:37-39);

6. And the sword of the Spirit; which is the Word of God. Jesus went to battle with "It is written." That is still the most effective way to do it. Forgetting the Word of God we have only our own fatally flawed wisdom to fall back on, and it will not do.

Can He who called you and me to this journey see us through?

Oh, yes! "The one who calls you is faithful and he will do it" (1 Thessalonians 5:24).

CHAPTER EIGHT

THE FREEDOM TO BE AND TO BECOME

Matthew 13:24-30

In Kenya I stood before a group of young girls—tall, slender, and beautiful Masai girls—who had been brought into a very special refugee center. They had been brought there for their own safety, and for education, for the healing of the mind and the body. They were aged between eight and twelve. They had been sold by their parents into marriage; not sold with the intention to be married in a few years. No, they were married. The Kenyan government is trying to put a stop to this abuse of children. I am told that when they first came to this center, run by your Seventh-day Adventist Church, they were so shy and timid they would not speak to you or look you in the eyes. They were children who had been robbed of their freedom—freedom to be and to become something more, something better, something greater. It

73

occurred to me that the church is meant to be a place of refuge for people battered and bruised by the experiences of life.

Jesus had much to say about how we relate to people. He could say the most amazing things! Things people were not used to hearing, certainly not from religious leaders. They were surprised; and I suppose a bit shocked. He seemed to read people like an open book. Really, quite uncanny! And He had the habit of telling stories to teach them whatever lessons were on His mind. The stories were memorable, and at times haunting. Jesus of Nazareth—there was no one quite like Him.

He had the remarkable gift of being open, generous, and receptive to people who were obviously full of mistakes, flawed as could be; and He did it without in the process destroying the clear lines of distinction between right and wrong, or implying that mistakes are inconsequential. Ordinary people, and that covers most of those who came, may have felt very inadequate and unworthy in His company, but they never felt rejected. And this is where He differed from most of us.

Most of us, when confronted with the shortcomings and mistakes of others, may be inclined to want to tell them off. We may feel the inner pressure of speeches of the "don'ts" and "you should not have" kind by which distances are established and people are made to feel inadequate, like failures—and are pushed away. We are often caught in the difficult tension between our relationships to issues and standards, on the one hand, and our relationships to people, on the other. I am unable to read the Gospels without being forcefully struck by the fact that, at the end of the day, it mattered enormously to the Lord Jesus how we treat people; that Jesus had more to say about relationship values; about what we do to each other, or should do but fail to, than He did in formulating dogmatic statements. It is on this matter of relationships within the church that I believe Jesus is seeking to say something in a story to which I find myself occasionally drawn.

The story is recorded in Matthew 13:24-30. It deals with some critical issues in regard to value judgments we sometimes make of one another, even in the same community of faith. There are some perplexing things this story confronts us with. We want to be sure that we have understood what He is getting at.

The background to the story that we are going to consider is probably found in the teachings of Jesus regarding His kingdom. He taught that the kingdom of God was to come, and yet the "kingdom is at hand." In a sense the kingdom had arrived, and the followers of Jesus were already here and now citizens of that kingdom, and, at least proleptically, they were experiencing in this life the blessings of the eternal kingdom.

But it was observed by many, and no doubt commented on by some, that the group of people who seemed to gather around Jesus on His goings and comings in Palestine was a very mixed lot—and some of them a bit disreputable. Granted there were some whose lives had clearly changed; one could see that. But then there were others who seemed distinctly out of place; and one wondered, and some may well have asked Him: "What are You going to do about this? Are You not going to have some screening and separate at least some of them out from Your followers? If this is what Your kingdom is made of—well, it's all a bit disgusting! I mean, look at them! When are You going to set Your house in order?" May I suggest that it is in answer to precisely such questions that Jesus told the story in Matthew 13?

Here is how Jesus told the story:

> "The kingdom of heaven may be compared to a man who sowed good seed in his field. But while men were sleeping, his enemy came and sowed tares also among the wheat, and went away. But when the wheat sprang up and bore grain, then the tares became evident also. And the slaves of the landowner came and said to him, 'Sir, did you

not sow good seed in your field? How then does it have tares?' And he said to them, 'An enemy has done this!' And the slaves said to him, 'Do you want us, then, to go and gather them up?' But he said, 'No; lest while you are gathering up the tares, you may root up the wheat with them. Allow both to grow together until the harvest; and in the time of the harvest I will say to the reapers, "First gather up the tares and bind them in bundles to burn them up; but gather the wheat into my barn" ' " (NASB).

The first thing we notice is that the owner of the field—and the field here is the church, or the community of believers—is not responsible for the presence of the tares, or the weed. It is just there, as a reality of life, an expression of the inevitable cross-section of humanity we find in the church. And we come to the heart of the story when Jesus answers this specific question: "What shall we do with the weed? Shall we remove it?" And to that He says clearly, "No, that would not be a good idea."

He does not even encourage the idea of just investigating to determine what is what. He is actually quite final about leaving it alone for the time being.

The story is unusual, for surely it would be normal to do what you can to deal with the weed and get rid of it somehow. But the Lord of the harvest says: "No, not now. I will take care of it Myself later." The wheat and the tares represent the mixed humanity that makes up our community, those who are "of the world" and those who are "of Christ." They have seemingly the same spiritual "sitz"—they grow up next to each other. And yet, some are good, and some are potentially very destructive.

Is not that humanity as you and I know it?

The parable says much about how the Lord views humanity, and about the realities of life in the church. Since we all claim Him as Lord and we belong to His spiritual family, we need to hear and understand what He says to us on this matter, for I think He says something important to us.

1. *The church is a very mixed lot.* I am not saying that that fact is either good or bad; I am just saying that that is reality; that is the way it is. And it will be like that until the Lord returns. Yes, I believe that through the Spirit's presence and workings the church will become a purer and holier community, and we will increase in commitment and devotion to Him as Lord, and we will become more useful to Him, and we will also learn from our past mistakes, and I myself will grow and hopefully become a better person. But I have little sympathy with those who maintain a doctrine of a pre-Advent infallible purging of the church that motivates them to initiate a process of uprooting tares at any cost, instead of leaving that difficult task to the work of the Spirit in the human heart. It is a fact of life that goodness and badness, saints and sinners, victory and defeat—yes, wheat and tares—are close neighbors. And therefore . . .

2. *You cannot always tell them apart* one from the other, and we should not engage ourselves on a mission to try to do that in too doctrinaire a manner, particularly when it comes to evaluating the lives of fellow travelers within the church.

And when the presence of the weed (the tares) is called to the attention of the landowner, he readily acknowledges, "Yes, it's true," and that the enemy is responsible. Well, they ask, shouldn't we deal with it, pull them up and throw them out, and in some final manner take care of these destructive elements? And the troublesome and challenging response of the Lord is: "No, do not go and weed in My garden; when the moment is right I will take care of it Myself."

The Landowner is not questioning, and nor am I, that there are people, possibly many, within the church, who are strangers to the Lord. They may at one time have known Him, but for one reason or another they have become weary of the walk, or they have lost sight of the goal, or have found other things or persons more interesting. And yet they stay, perhaps because they find it convenient, or more secure, or because a job is at stake, or because of family issues; or just simply because it is less embarrassing to continue to occupy space in the pew than it would be to leave. These are the sad realities. To these realities the Lord says: "Leave them be. To ostracize them, or freeze them out, or for you, as the keepers of the garden, to go on a general cleaning-up exercise, is not a good idea. I will do it Myself in My own time. For you to do it is fraught with too many risks."

You may ask: "What do you mean that the risks are too many or too great or too high?" In answering this question we must acknowledge values that are sacred to humanity, values we cannot infringe on without damaging ourselves, one another, and our communities. These are self-evident and inalienable rights. These are values that I believe our Lord wants us to respect. Freedom, with all its unsettling potentials, is one of them. Even the freedom to go astray.

So you do not misunderstand me, I must differentiate between what I believe the Lord is trying to teach us in this story, and the flagrant abuse of the church's identity, standards, and mission by someone who ostensibly claims to belong to the church but who is increasingly showing himself or herself hostile and destructive to the church, its message, and its mission. Such a person does not belong. The church has a right to say so and take actions to signify that. We call that "church discipline." It is always sad when that has to happen, but also that is a course the Scripture signifies as being necessary on some occasions. That fact, however, must not skew the greater reality and much more frequently occurring phenomenon of day-to-day interrelationships in which spiritual high-handedness is manifested.

But back to the question: Why are the risks too high? They are too high first *because of my own humanity*. Am I, as the spiritual guardian of the church, all-knowing? Is it not possible that I might make a terrible mistake in assessing another person? Do I really think that I know fully and accurately what goes on inside another person? Surely only God knows. And is it not possible that when an individual becomes difficult in the church—obstreperous and rebellious—and particularly if that individual is a teenager, is it not possible that the behavior occurs precisely because God, somehow, is getting through to them and touching their lives? God only knows how much latitude He will put up with. I don't.

Second, *today is still the day of salvation*. We may have been able to accurately identify and label the "tare" and isolate it, but we must not forget that God has not yet finished His work.

Again, let me clarify. I am not talking about those in our churches who are openly abusing and flagrantly defying the standards of the Word of God and of the church, and who must for their own salvation's sake be placed under church discipline. Of that the Bible speaks clearly. I am talking about the much larger number of persons who are not that easy to identify, and who may be spending their time on the brink of the kingdom of God. We have many youth who disappear from the church because they were made to feel unworthy and unwelcome in the church. We made them feel spiritually unsuccessful. The church is saying to them: "God does not like you very much!" We presume to know the mind of God too readily! Is it possible that God is more generous than we are?

Listen to these words from the inspired pen of Ellen White:

Although in our churches, that claim to believe advanced truth, there are those who are faulty and erring, as tares among the wheat, God is long-suffering and patient. . . . He does not destroy those who are long in learning the lesson He would teach them. . . .

The church of Christ on earth will be imperfect, but God does not destroy His church because of its imperfection. . . . There is to be no spasmodic, zealous, hasty action taken by church members in cutting off those they may think defective in character (Ellen G. White, *Testimonies to Ministers,* pp. 45, 46).

And one more:

"I warn the Seventh-day Adventist Church to be careful how you receive every new notion and those who claim to have great light. The character of their work seems to be to accuse and tear down" (Ellen G. White, *Selected Messages,* 2:69).

Is it possible that God might be warning against anyone's zealous but misguided intrusion into the space and freedom that God has given to each human being? Even when their exercise of that freedom leads them to wrong choices even with respect to God Himself—or at least, so they seem to me?

Third, the risk is too high because *the church herself is harmed by people probing even delicately into and having opinions about the lives of other people.* And our lives are so intertwined that the damage can spread very widely. The climate can become such that even good people are made to feel insecure in their own spiritual home, and the whole lifestyle of the church becomes cramped. Something terrible happens to the church. The church is meant to be a place where people feel at home, warm and wanted, safe, secure, accepted, and free. Instead, the church community becomes a most unpleasant place.

Fourth, weeding in the garden is too risky because *I, the investigator, am myself harmed* by these activities. My misguided "mission" alters my own character, and my personality becomes unattractive. By going around and actively nurturing opinions about the quality of other people's spirituality, something happens to me. And if you don't think so, just look around. I am reminded of the words of a former teacher of mine to a man who was being "hard" on being right, and somewhat self-congratulatory of his own accomplishments: "So you are perfect, but do you have to be hostile about it?"

What kind of spiritual climate are we creating in our churches? If your church is not the most appealing and attractive spiritual fellowship in your community, what are you going to do to change that?

Our churches are meant to be places of healing and renewal. They must be:

1. Attractive places for the *unbelievers* to be drawn to; must reflect values and an appealing quality of human relationships that can fill the void that many feel and struggle with how to fill;

2. A place where the *believer* feels at home, secure, free, and accepted. Not a battlefield, but a city of refuge, which was also God's design. Can that be said of the church in which you and I worship?

Or is the spirit in your church different?

I am concerned about the spirit we maintain in our churches. Our churches are not to be an exclusive club for those who are good enough or worthy enough. It is sinners that God is constantly justifying, and they are never good enough. They are meant to be received warmly in our churches, for that is their rightful home. I will be frank with you: I would hate to spend my time surrounded only by people who thought that they had everything worked out just right. They become arrogant, clinical, and judgmental of those who still have a lot of growing to do, and acceptance by *them* is always conditional on whether you will respond constructively to *their* instructions on how you should shape your life. And yet Christ accepted us all "while we were yet sinners" (Romans 5:8). Acceptance is the breath of humanity. Where acceptance is denied, our breathing falters. The air becomes thin, and life itself becomes unbearable!

But this is not easy. As responsible church leaders we know and at times feel the tensions between the things we should deal with in the church and the things we somehow must allow to stay; or that we must leave with the Lord to find His own time or a better way to deal with. We as church leaders are human; we love the Lord, we love the church and the truth, we are jealous and protective of these, but also we belong to fallen humanity, and we may not get it right always.

Our being jealous for the truth and the Lord must not lead us to intrude or invade the space and freedom that are moments or opportunities for an individual to become something other than what he or she is now. These are opportunities God gives to each human being. That fundamental freedom must be respected.

I am reminded of another story told by our Lord in Luke 13:6-8.

"A man had a fig tree, planted in his vineyard, and he went to look for fruit on it, but did not find any. So he said to the man who took care of the vineyard, 'For three years now I've been coming to look for fruit on this fig tree and haven't found any. Cut it down! Why should it use up the soil?' 'Sir,' the man replied, 'leave it alone for one more year, and I'll dig around it and fertilize it. If it bears fruit next year, fine! If not, then cut it down.' "

It is within our reach to create and shape the spiritual environment of our communities for the future. My appeal is that we create a good home for the future in which people can communicate, understand each other, respect each other's space, and acknowledge that the Lord is ever at work making something better out of what is flawed.

CHAPTER NINE

SUCCEEDING WHATEVER HAPPENS

Ecclesiastes 7:13-22

A number of years have now passed, but I remember the incident as though it were yesterday: A man was severely beaten up by muggers who left him for dead. He was taken into hospital in a serious condition. His aged father, who, like his son, was a devout Christian, came to see his son and prayed for him in the presence of the nurses. He prayed that God would watch over him and that God's will be done in his life. As the old man left the hospital he said to the nurses that his son would be safe in God's hands.

Two weeks later the injured man died. The believing father, we were told, asserted without hesitation that it was not the will of the heavenly Father that his son should die; this was the act of the evil one, and God should not be blamed for what had happened.

Your life surely has parallels to this story:

- You pray for a safe journey and believe that the Lord has control; and yet it ends in tragedy.
- You pray for healing, believing that the heavenly Healer is mighty to do it, and yet recovery does not come.
- You pray for your wayward children, believing that the Lord loves them more than you do, and that He can reach them, and yet they seem to drift further away.

Does He not care? Is He deaf? Am I so evil that He will not listen to me, and even if I were, why should He take it out on the one who needs His help and for whom I am praying? If God is able to do, but doesn't act, has He not got an ethical problem?

It is a wonderful gift of faith to be able to hold together the two thoughts that (1) we are totally submitted to and trusting of God's will, and at the same time (2) what happens is not the expression of the will of God but of the evil one. It is a gift of faith to accept that the presence of God does not take away the pain, but it helps us through it; that as one weeps at the grave of a son, God is there weeping also.

It may seem a contradiction to assert that we are submitting to God's will and yet at the same time say that what happens is not the will of God. But it is no contradiction. The fact is that the two thoughts point to a trust and loyalty to God which says that you cannot go wrong whatever happens. It says that I am on God's side and He is on mine, and at least ultimately that is a winning combination.

Do you find God easy to understand? Can you readily figure Him out?

I find His ways often unsearchable. But I find that traveling with Him through life is safe. He knows what awaits me around the corner, and He can handle whatever it is. He can be trusted. Not because His ways are so ingeniously or cleverly carved into my future, but because God Himself is good.

Ecclesiastes 7:13-22 expresses in part what I am trying to say, but it does not say it very clearly. It hints at some important points, and it paints the picture in bold strokes. There are four thoughts that come to me from this passage.

First, don't think you can figure God out by your own simple understanding of what you think is ideal. Don't make God's way of acting or responding to a given situation too predictable. You will be confused and frustrated. Your own simplified "cause and effect" formula will let you down if you apply it to God. Being close to God and praying daily does not lead to health instead of illness; it does not mean that you will pass an exam rather than fail it; it does not help you to find a job rather than being unemployed; and it does not help you being elected in rather than being elected out.

Remarkably, says the wise man, "God has made the one as well as the other. Therefore, a man cannot discover anything about his future"; or as *The New English Bible* has it, He sets one "alongside the other in such a way that no one can find out what is going to happen next" (verse 14).

God is outside the predictable formula of cause and effect.

Some righteous men, women, and children die early living good lives, but some evil ones go on and on. It does not seem fair. But God says, For the time being that's how life is.

You may have heard the story of Joanne Gillespie. She had been diagnosed with a cancerous brain tumor and given six months to live. But she became a celebrity in England, where she lived, because of her refusal to give in, and she wrote two books about her fight before she succumbed to her illness. She was fifteen years old. Some of her inner qualities shone through in a poem she wrote that was read by her twelve-year-old sister at her funeral:

> THANKS
> Thanks God for listening to me all those times I wanted to talk to you. Even though I go on a bit.
> Thanks for helping me when I asked. And thanks for laughter.
> Thank you God for Michael Jackson, loud music, ballet and snowflakes.
> For strawberries and doctors and snowmen and scarecrows. And even some dentists!
> Thank you for families and friends and all the things I don't understand. Though some may be painful, like war and death and hunger. I still thank you because you are giving me the chance to help others.
> And when it is time to put away all things you gave me, please God don't let me say "Why?" Let me say "Thanks."

The second thought from Ecclesiastes 7 is "Don't be over-righteous, neither be overwise" (verse 16). To most of us that sounds like bad advice, it sounds very strange, and most unlike something God would say. Both righteousness and wisdom are, elsewhere in Scripture, lifted high as something to be sought. Could it be that we are here being warned against something very specific? I think so.

First, we are being warned against losing touch with the realities of everyday life, with its ups and downs. Also in the life of a believer, as we know well, victories and defeats are constant companions. Beware of the kind of enthusiasm that denies this reality. And so the wise man says: "There is not a righteous man on earth who does what is right always and can never do wrong" (see verse 20).

From time to time we meet individuals whose preoccupation with the score sheets of their own lives is such that they are unable safely to tell their own state. Some think they have reached perfection and that sin is no longer a factor to be reckoned with in their lives; others believe that they are hopelessly lost. They look at their lives and become terribly discouraged. Standards of right and wrong are being abused, and one feels terrible. And one wonders, *What's the point of going on? I am not going to make it.* We can be so hard and unforgiving with ourselves, and we allow ourselves to come adrift simply because we cannot see a respectable way back. We have disappointed ourselves and too many other people. We are too embarrassed, and it is difficult to see the point of even trying.

So let me tell you: We all carry baggage from yesterday. The sack of guilt on our shoulders can be very heavy. And we don't like ourselves very much. I am reminded of one of David Kossoff's chats with the Lord:

> Help me, Lord, to be free of the sack (of guilt).
> If not entirely free, to empty it a little.
> Help me to like myself a bit more.
> I tell you, Lord,
> One or two people think I am not so bad.
> And on a good day I can also stand me.
> But most of the time, Lord, I could weep
> (David Kossoff, *You Have a Minute, Lord,* p. 61).

So, my message is, Don't let the burden weigh you down so you cannot walk upright. The wonderful but simple meaning of repentance is that we are given the opportunity to start again.

As far as Christ is concerned, if your repentance is genuine count it as a new day and a fresh start with Him. "Why destroy yourself?" The Lord has a lot more sympathy and understanding for those who find the journey difficult and the weight of the sack heavy than we extend to each other. That is why He said: "Come to Me all of you who carry a heavy weight, and I will lighten your load." Christ is not an enemy—He is not a spy, He is not a gossip, He is not an intruder, He is not a watchdog. He is just a Friend. The tenth beatitude, which is not spelled out in the list but which the Gospels breathe, is "Blessed are the ones who don't quite make it, and who know it, for they are never forgotten by the Lord."

Second, there is a warning: "Don't think that you have got everything worked out to a fine system."

Whilst textbook theology knows a lot and systematic theology is a good way of summarizing our biblical findings, beware of any theology or any theologian who claims to have the final and definitive word on any and all matters. Said the wise man: "Do not be overwise." We have so much still to learn, even about what we think we understand, to say nothing of what we readily confess is a mystery.

Greatness of mind and humility go together. A great mind is not one that is keen to display how much it knows but has the humility to confess how much it has yet to learn.

The third thought is from Ecclesiastes 7:18, and it has a mixed reading. The NEB says, "The man who fears God will succeed both ways." The NIV says, "A man who fears God will avoid all [extremes]"; and in the footnote: "Or 'will follow them both,' " coming close to the reading in the NEB.

Whatever the reading should be, there is much to be said for both of the thoughts expressed. The "man who fears God will avoid all [extremes]." The life of a believer is a balanced life.

You don't become a fanatic, nor do you spend time so far out in left field that you don't know the difference between right and wrong. A person who fears God is neither constantly looking for excuses nor is he or she judgmental. Just generous and helpful.

I want to come back to the wording in the NEB: "A man who fears God will succeed both ways." What does it mean to succeed both ways? The wise man has just been talking about not being overrighteous, or overwise, or overwicked, or overfoolish. In "A man who fears God will succeed both ways," the phrase "both ways" means *whatever happens*. Success in God's vocabulary and in God's view of the world is not as obvious as we may think. It is not as predictable a course with as predictable results here and now as we may tend to make it. Nor is God as numbers- and statistics-orientated as we are inclined to be. God has the ability and the right to turn on its head many a thing that we may call success and call it failure, and *vice versa*. Who is to say that a young man who fails to pass his exam but finds the resources and motivation to turn his life around has not succeeded? Who is to say that the young woman who fails to hold the man who was her first choice but who nevertheless puts together a good life for herself and for others has failed? Who is to say that the young marriage where one of the partners strayed where he or she should not have gone cannot succeed? Success with God is possible even in the most awkward, strained, and difficult situations.

Think of the church in our mission: How do we know whether we have succeeded or failed? Oh, we are quite good at numbering Israel, and possibly we think that the impressive figures tell of our success. Have we forgotten that at one time God warned against numbering Israel? God is best at adding up His own sums, for at the end of the day they are truly *His* sums.

89

One of the greatest challenges we face as a church in terms of our mission is, How are we expected to complete God's mission among the Muslims? What does God expect of us in terms of bringing a witness to people confined within the restrictive world of Islam? Will it do just leaving a witness there? Must you be able to statistically measure the impact of God's mission there for you to allow yourself to think in terms of success? The Spirit is infinitely able to pick up the witness we leave behind and work wonders and miracles with it, the final results of which we may not know until we are in the kingdom.

I have said many a time that I believe God is extremely versatile. He works with many options. If one does not work God will try something else, and something else again. Even as we pray to God, He does not bind our hands in terms of the choices we then proceed to make. Sometimes I believe He could wish that we had chosen differently, but He allows us the latitude to make our choices even as He sits among us. And He may well say: "This time you have made it more difficult for Me, but I will work with the choices you have made." And if we stay with Him He will work with us, and we will succeed either way.

The decisive factor in determining whether what we are doing will be successful lies in what the writer calls "fearing God." ("A man who fears God will succeed both ways.") And immediately the focus shifts away from statistics, systems, courses, curricula, and score sheets, or from anything that is performance focused, to what is called "fearing God." What does it mean to "fear God"?

Some people are afraid of God, but this passage is not about fright or alarm or terror. Rather it has to do with taking God seriously—with treating Him as an important and decisive factor in my life. It has to do with accepting that He is a *real Person* to me, not just a statement in some book or from some pulpit; it has to do with making a deliberate choice in favor of God. It has to do with saying to myself and to Him: I am going to do something personally about Him. I will talk to Him. And I will walk with Him. I will ask Him to help me sort out my life. I will not plan to seek in my life what I know is alien to Him. That is what it means to fear God.

We said earlier that God's ways are not always easy to figure out. Well, fearing God means that you will not suspend loyalty to Him until you have fully figured Him out. It means that I will not suspend loyalty to Him simply because I have to confess with some frustration that my system of theology is somewhat incomplete, or because I find myself confessing what my understanding is still having a struggle with. I don't understand it all; I confess that there are times when I have to say I don't know. But I am going to trust God also when I don't understand. That is my position. This is where I stand. I am confused and at times I see only through a very darkened glass, but I see enough to know that God is with me, and that is what matters. I feel safe. Yes, I am His. We belong together.

As for the idea of suspending loyalty to God as a person in your life until you see everything clearly, forget it! You never will, and without God you will only become more confused. Together you will succeed whatever happens.

The fourth thought from Ecclesiastes 7 is this: Please, do not become paranoid about your failures and shortcomings. The world contains no man or woman, professor or student, professional or dropout, who is so righteous that they do right always and never wrong.

Sometimes we meet people who make huge claims about themselves and their ability to put it together right always. Well, don't let them intimidate you by their superior claims and speeches. Some people are blind, others are liars, and then there are those who are just plain stupid. I am reminded of the story of the poet who also sadly happened to be a heavy drinker. He couldn't maintain his steady walk, and he toppled over into the ditch by the country lane. One of the upright men of the neighborhood walked by and stopped long enough to give him a stern and condemning lecture on the folly of his life. The poet answered: "I am drunk, but that will pass. But you are stupid, and that will never pass." I am not suggesting that the poet had found any wisdom, but pompous and superior lectures do not help anyone.

And the one who never experiences doubts in regard to matters of faith and doctrine has probably stopped thinking. It is amazing, but some people are capable of occupying space for years on end without their gray cells being engaged in a single new or creative thought. And they are critical of those who are.

So Ecclesiastes says, Don't destroy yourself because you recognize some failures in your life or because you have days when doubts unsettle you. That is the way life is. Most of us are much more severe on ourselves than God is.

So, what is God actually saying to us? What does God expect of each of us? What does God want of us?

Put simply, God says, I want you to be holy. "Desires for . . . true holiness are right so far as they go; but if you stop here, they will avail nothing. . . . Many will be lost while hoping and desiring to be Christians; but they made no earnest effort, therefore they will be weighed in the balances and found wanting" (Ellen G. White, *Testimonies for the Church,* 2:265, 266). God says, I want you to belong to Me, and I want that to be seen; I want to put My identity on the values you choose and on the way you conduct your lives.

God says, I want you to know that I care very deeply and profoundly for you; so I want you to trust Me. I never forget you.

And, He says, I want you to do rather better at being human beings; I want you to be kinder and more considerate toward people you meet.

And to underline it all, numerous passages of Scripture jump out at us: "Remind the people . . . to be ready to do whatever is good, to slander no one, to be peaceable and considerate, and to show true humility toward all men" (Titus 3:1, 2). "Make every effort to live in peace with all men and to be holy" (Hebrews 12:14; cf. 2 Timothy 1:12). Through the prophet Micah God put it another way: You know what the Lord requires of you, "to act justly and to love mercy and to walk humbly with your God" (Micah 6:8). Do that, and you come out right. The one who fears God will succeed whatever happens.

CHAPTER TEN

REACHING FOR A BETTER HUMANITY

Psalm 103:8-14; Colossians 3:12-14

In this morning hour
The world listens to itself,

To the things that people like us are doing
To each other.
We shake our heads and wonder
What the world is coming to
And whether it is possible
To be forgiven for what we have done.
Lord of life, help us.

Forgiveness is what we need
For the grudges we hold,

For the thoughts we think,
For the words we say,
For the things we do . . .
For guns and bombs
For the savage destruction
That man has wreaked for centuries;
Lord of life, help us.

You Lord are the God of mercy,
The forgiving God,
The giver of peace,
And peace of mind is what we need . . .
The peace that comes from mutual forgiveness—
Peace in our homes,
Peace in our hearts,
Peace in the world
(Frank Topping, *Pause for Thought,* pp. 41, 42).

A Yugoslavian Serb, looking pensively at the river Danube as it slowly flows past him through Belgrade, says, more to himself than to anyone else, "During the Second World War the Croats, allied with the Nazis, killed half a million Serbs, and their bodies came floating down on this river from Croatia. We will never forget, and we will never forgive them for that." And his mind drifts off into the murky haze of a history of realities and myths.

Have I not said—have you not thought: "I will never forgive"? Never?

Can I find peace with myself and the people that surround me if I cannot or will not forgive? We are all going to be wronged, hurt, or abused sometime; that's the way life is. What do we plan to do about it? How do we handle it?

Whenever Jesus wanted to make a significant point or teach a lesson of great importance He told a story. These stories describe the realities of everyday life, then and today, in which people often hurt each other, and then often throw a religious cloak over it all thereby managing also to distort God.

Most of these stories said something about relationships— between one human being and another, or between God and human beings. And they sought to drive home the point that we need somehow to do better than we are at just being human beings. We need to discover what the finest human qualities are. The discovery starts when we ask, How does God look upon people? How does He value a human being? And does this say something about how I should look upon and treat the people I meet on my journey through life?

The predominant quality of God that says more than any other about God's attitude to people is His willingness to forgive. And the presence or absence of precisely this quality is what creates or destroys relationships between people. Jesus taught, Freely you have received, and, therefore, equally freely you are expected to give (see Matthew 10:8). One day one of the disciples said to Jesus, "Lord, how often would You think I should forgive someone who goes on abusing me, offending me, and in many ways doing me wrong? I know I don't have to sit there and just take it; I can walk away. But, Lord, the question of forgiveness does arise. What would You think—seven times?"

"No, more like seventy times seven."

It is not the arithmetic that is flawed, it is the mind-set. Reaching for a better humanity moves us away from any notion of "an eye for an eye" or score settling or "how many times has who done what to whom."

It is somehow easier to judge than it is to forgive; to point a finger; to shake the head, even as I sit insecurely perched on the self-made mountain of my own mistakes. And the sins I condemn the most in others are those that echo mine. "Lord, do I have the humility and grace to recognize myself in the frailty of others?"

A serious comment from the pen of inspiration—listen to this:

> He who is unforgiving cuts off the very channel through which alone he can receive mercy from God. We should not think that unless those who have injured us confess the wrong we are justified in withholding from them our forgiveness. It is their part, no doubt, to humble their hearts by repentance and confession; but we are to have a spirit of compassion toward those who have trespassed against us, whether or not they confess their faults. However sorely they may have wounded us, we are not to cherish our grievances and sympathize with ourselves over our injuries; but as we hope to be pardoned for our offenses against God we are to pardon all who have done evil to us (Ellen G. White, *Thoughts From the Mount of Blessing*, p. 113).

Tall order? Yes, but this is God saying to me, through His inspired servant, "This is how I want you to live life."

God is in the habit of being very direct. "Be kind and compassionate to one another, forgiving each other, just as in Christ God forgave you" (Ephesians 4:32).

One of the stories Jesus told particularly drives home the importance of the point I am making. It is recorded in Matthew 18:23-35. We meet a high-ranking steward in the king's service who had built up a huge debt with his master. The debt was, as far as we can tell, way beyond his ability to settle. He was hopelessly sunk, and there was no way he could redeem himself. The debt he owed was so large that we cannot conceive of it in monetary terms—"ten thousand talents." Ten thousand was the highest figure used in reckoning, and a talent was the largest monetary denomination. Simply put, the figure is beyond grasp. Even so, the servant kids himself. He thinks he can pay it back given a bit of time, and that is all he asks for—time. But his master sees the hopelessness of his situation, and he takes pity on him. The master knows that this irresponsible steward cannot repay the debt he had recklessly accrued, and he cancels the debt. Mercy and compassion override all other considerations.

But it does not end there. We meet a parallel incident with one or two major differences. The servant who has just had his debt forgiven meets a fellow servant who owes him what by comparison is a pittance. He threatens him, and when he is not able to repay his debt immediately he has him cast into a prison. Yes, there was a difference in the size of the debt, but the greatest difference was in the spirit. When the master gets wind of this he calls in the servant and says to him: "You useless, contemptible creature. Didn't I just forgive you a huge debt because you begged me to? Shouldn't you have shown some mercy to one of your colleagues to reflect the kindness I had extended to you?" That is God's question to you and me as we journey out into life! You and I will surely meet our own version of this scenario.

We find in this story a message of warning and judgment. It teaches a lesson that runs through the whole of the New Testament: To receive forgiveness from God, I must be willing to forgive. To be treated with compassion, I must be willing to be generous to other people. Divine forgiveness and human forgiveness are interlocked and cannot be separated.

Said Jesus in the fifth beatitude, "Blessed are those who show mercy, for mercy shall be shown to them." And: "If you forgive men when they sin against you, your heavenly Father will also forgive you. But if you do not, you are on your own." (See Matthew 6:14, 15.) Or, in the words of James, "Judgment without mercy will be shown to anyone who has not been merciful. Mercy triumphs over judgment!" (James 2:13).

But you can only truly forgive someone who has wronged you if you have some sense of compassion for that individual and a degree of understanding for that person who now has wronged you. The sentiment is well described by the psalmist:

"The Lord is gracious and compassionate, slow to anger and rich in love. The Lord is good to all; he has compassion on all he has made" (Psalm 145:8, 9).

And it is precisely here that most of us fail so miserably.

"It is most difficult, even for those who claim to be followers of Jesus, to forgive as Christ forgives us. The true spirit of forgiveness is so little practiced, and so many interpretations are placed upon Christ's requirement, that its force and beauty are lost sight of" (Ellen G. White, *That I May Know Him,* p. 180).

Compassion and understanding make for a better humanity; it simply is a better way to start a day and to nurture any relationship. Humanly speaking it proceeds from an acknowledgment that we are frail and at some fault; and we don't have to pretend otherwise. Compassion is important because it changes us as individuals. Compassion stands apart from the continuous traffic between good and evil within me. What would you rather be governed by, a clumsy and maybe not-so-gifted leader who has the capacity to understand and show some pity, or an efficient technocrat whose dedication to the letter of the law (or policy) makes him or her cold and somewhat brutal?

There are times when it is better to be kind than it is to be right! I say this to people who are accustomed to placing a high premium on being "right."

Compassion and mercy grow out of some heartfelt understanding for the other person's misfortune and distress. It has to do with taking the time and energy to become involved in the suffering and misfortune of someone else. Compassion cannot be entertained at a distance. And maybe for that very reason understanding and compassion are somewhat rare. To entertain and express these sentiments you have to allow people to get close to you—often closer than comfort wants; and you must allow yourself to be pulled into their lives. It demands time and it is often emotionally exhausting. But it is a good way of living life.

It is a wonderful fact that when you have met someone who understands you—who has helped you to lift the burden and you are able to walk out of the darkness of despair and loneliness—the attraction of bearing grudges and passing judgment is somehow not the same anymore. Remember Paul's words: Love "keeps no record of wrongs" (1 Corinthians 13:5). "Praise be to the God and Father of our Lord Jesus Christ, the Father of compassion and the God of all comfort, who comforts us in all our troubles, so that we can comfort those in any trouble with the comfort we ourselves have received from God" (2 Corinthians 1:3, 4).

As we journey through life we will meet individuals who may not have been schooled by the best institutions and who may not have the right to add letters after their names, but who have a special gift in their ability to understand people. And they find time to make the effort. They are often on the quiet side, observant and perceptive. They listen more than they speak, and you sense that they have time for you. Sometime they will surprise you not by their cleverness, but by the depth of their insight. They are healers; they understand.

To really be able to understand someone you have to be willing not just to step into his or her shoes, but you also have to be willing to walk around in them for a while. I am reminded of the words of Soren Kierkegaard:

> For the rights of understanding to be valid one must venture out into life . . . and not only stand and watch others fighting and struggling—only then does understanding acquire its official sanction, for to stand on one leg and prove God's existence is a very different thing from going on one's knees and thanking him (*The Journals of Kierkegaard,* p. 68).

Understanding another does not mean condoning the wrongs that that person has done, but it also means that I, in the statements I make to and about that person, do not behave as though I am God.

Probably one of the greatest gifts that any human being can give to another is to make the effort to try to understand that person. It is important to know that you have someone to whom you can go at any time and know that they will not laugh at your dreams, your hopes, and your failures; and to know that they will not misuse your confidence; you will not be left feeling naked. It is good to have someone to whom you can go and find the tensions of life relax—to find peace. It requires no lavish surroundings and no costly entertainment. It just requires a bit of time and interest.

Now, how does this tie in with the parable with which we began? The parable was about forgiveness. Forgiveness leads to closeness rather than distance, to understanding rather than indifference, to healing rather than hurt.

The parable is surrounded by a number of questions: What are the limits that I can justifiably hold to in relationships with a person who has done me wrong? "How many times, Lord, do You reasonably expect me to forgive my colleague? My room-mate? My son? My husband? Lord, knowing the gravity of what has happened, surely You do not expect me to go on and on and on? Where can I reasonably draw the line? When is enough enough?"

The questions all have this in common: They think in terms of limits. "Surely there comes a reasonable point at which I can say: It is enough. I have to be able to draw the line somewhere. Surely even God does that—doesn't He?"

The answer really has to do with the depth and strength of your love. The answer to this type of thinking is simply to accept that charity does not look for limits; it looks for opportunities. Love does not constantly have a need to qualify itself. How often should I forgive? The question itself is wrong. It has nothing to do with times. It has to do with mind-set. It has to do with learning to be a better human being.

The rabbis had a saying that went something like this: "A man whose knowing exceeds his doing is like a tree with many branches but few roots." There is something ominous about that, wouldn't you say?

I look at myself and my people and I ponder: Do we have much knowledge? Yes, quite a bit. Much understanding of doc-trines? Oh, yes, and the arguments and proofs are often unas-sailable. Policies to cover all eventualities? Oh, yes, and usually tightly reasoned and well written.

What troubles me about all of this is that on their own, within the covers of a document or a book, there is not much life in them. And our Lord nowhere commends such a collec-tion of opinions and factual arrangements. On the contrary He says that anyone who has these theories well worked out, but does not act in relationships and behavior accordingly is " 'like a foolish man who built his house on sand . . . and it fell with a great crash' " (Matthew 7:26, 27).

The wonderful thing is that it does not have to be like that. There is a better humanity to be reached for, and you can find it. You just have to care enough to make the effort. Life becomes so much richer, the air so much purer and easier to breathe. That is what God expects of you and me as His children.

"This is how we know who the children of God are . . . Anyone who does not do what is right is not a child of God; nor is anyone who does not love his brother" (1 John 3:10).

A nun in Mother Teresa's community in Calcutta, no doubt influenced by that well-known prayer of St. Francis, penned these words:

> Lord, when I am hungry, send me someone in need of food;
> When I am thirsty, someone who needs water;
> When I am cold, someone who needs to be warmed;
> When I am hurt, someone in need of healing.
> When my cross becomes heavy to carry, Lord,
> Send me someone whose cross I can help to carry;
> When I am poor, send me someone in need;
> When I am too busy, someone who needs a few moments of my time;
> When I have been humbled, send me someone I can praise; and
> When I need to be understood, send me someone who needs my understanding.

It is a difficult prayer to live, yes, but it is worth the effort!

CHAPTER ELEVEN

CORDS OF HUMAN KINDNESS

Hosea 11:4; Philippians 2:1-5

The Lord desires me to call the attention of His people to the thirteenth chapter of First Corinthians. Read this chapter every day, and from it obtain comfort and strength. . . . Learn that Christlike love is of heavenly birth, and that without it all other qualifications are worthless (Ellen G. White Supplement, *SDA Bible Commentary*, 6:1091).

But we do not read it daily, and most of us reflect on its message only seldom. For the fact is that the love of which 1 Corinthians 13 speaks is a stranger and an enigma even among God's people. The word itself is confusing; it has been brandished in such a way by our cultures and our societies that the "diamonds" that lie sparkling in this chapter seem unreal and unattainable.

Love takes its meaning from God, not from the street, not from the movie industry, not from the glossy magazines. God says, Understanding love is very important, so let Me define it for you. And in order for you to be able to love each other, the first thing you must know about love is that it "comes from God. . . . Whoever does not love does not know God, because God is love" (1 John 4:7, 8).

So, clearly we are here talking about something that lies at the very heart of being a believer—a child of God!

Sometimes we are devious, we are angry, and we harbor evil plans about another person. We seize the occasion to destroy, at least verbally. At other times we are just clumsy, or awkward, or quick-tempered, or insensitive, and we come across even to those we love the most as being uncaring and not a very nice person. I said the wrong thing last night, I used harsh words, and my child weeps, or my spouse, my very best friend is deeply hurt. But inside I weep also, for I know that I hurt someone I love very much, but somehow I find it so difficult to say, "I'm sorry." I have failed my God, I have failed the one I love most, and I have failed myself. We all know the feeling; we are all part of the human family.

The Bible, we are told, has different words translated as *love* in our English Bibles. They carry meanings ranging from the highest principles of value and conduct to a very basic burst of hormones with hearts beating out of control. And I am far from sure that one can slice *love* into separable units each neatly labeled. In any case, as for me, I don't do very well when I am divided into "sections" of behavior. I do best as one whole person with passions and principles bursting forth from the same person, so we are going to deal with *love* as a broad statement of value and conduct that contains both passions and conduct.

Even so I know that there are differences between the affection I hold for a friend, for my children, for my wife, for my work, for ideas and values, and for my church; for the notion of love as passion and as a noble principle. We love our children and our partners, and we are also told to love our enemies. And obviously there is a difference; there had better be. But fundamentally—at least that is my experience—all notions of love come together in the capacity to care deeply or profoundly for anyone or anything. Do you—do I have that capacity?

Sometimes I meet people who become concerned that when one focuses on love, somehow other important things that are central to our lives as believers, such as the reading of the Word, obedience, and discipleship, are all devalued. They feel that faith somehow becomes very mushy and that worship is reduced to the singing of rhythmic songs with religious words. The worry is unwarranted. All the elements of doctrine and understanding that shape and define our faith are in place and are secure. But God's love for people is the driving force in everything that God seeks to accomplish with you and me. So, the love of God draws me like a powerful magnet.

When I read about God's love, as it comes to me from the prophet Hosea, it leaves me utterly speechless. It is so strong and overwhelming! There is the picture of God wooing back His unfaithful wife, Israel, with a love that is absolutely unfathomable. He says of Israel, "When you were a child in Egypt, when you walked the streets of your city, when you were sniffing, and smoking, and drinking what you should not, when you rebelled against your parents, your church, and Me, I loved you so much. And yet, somehow, the more I loved you the further you removed yourself from Me." (Does this sound familiar as you think of one of your own loved ones?) "And yet I held you in My arms and led you 'with cords of human kindness. I lifted the weight from your shoulders; I bent down to feed you' " (see Hosea 11). And God exposes the weight of His love for His children when He says, " 'How can I give you up, Ephraim [or Tom, or Janet]? How can I hand you over, Israel?' " (verse 8). " 'I have loved you with an everlasting love;

I have drawn you with loving-kindness' " (Jeremiah 31:3). This is the language of the powerfully committed love that God has for each of us. God cares deeply for what happens to each of us!

So, I ask you, Can you take it? Do you have the courage to let this divine love unimpeded access to your life? If you do, it will change you. You will become a different person. Every choice you make will become conditioned by it.

God says to me in Romans 12:10, "Honor one another above yourselves." And in 1 Peter 3:9, "Do not repay evil with evil or insult with insult."

These are not philosophical concepts. They are practical, down-to-earth advice about relationships. And, says God, the first place this love must find expression is in the family—between husbands and wives, between parents and children. There is no room for violence in the family or abuse between spouses or between parents and children. Someone has said that the greatest gift you as a father can give to your son is to love his mother! As spouses and as parents we are the makers and breakers of love in the family. And, yet, some family units are like iceboxes; and members of the family are driven elsewhere in confusion, looking for love, and often having to settle for substitutes.

Pause for a while and reflect on what 1 Corinthians 13 is saying to us. First look at the setting of this chapter. In chapters 12 and 14 Paul deals with a variety of spiritual gifts, and chapter 13 may at a quick glance seem like a parenthesis in the midst of an otherwise important presentation of gifts of the Spirit. But it is not an excursion or parenthesis; it is the heart of the matter. Love is the one indispensable gift that gives worth to every other gift. Lack that and every other gift or attribute you may have acquired is a waste.

Corinth was not an easy assignment! Yes, there were many spiritual gifts in the church, but the church was also tearing herself apart with spiritual people measuring each other's spirituality, and comparing each other's spiritual gifts; and they were going around creating feelings of spiritual inferiority and superiority. Paul looks at the church and sees in it a divided community, with people looking with suspicion and envy on each other, unable to love.

Paul's answer to this is simple: We need each other, he says. Let us not burn ourselves out in feelings of envy, suspicion, and superiority. We belong to each other and we are meant to live together. We have much to give and to receive from each other; and the one who refuses to receive from another's spiritual experience has no one with whom to share his or her own. And when that happens to an individual that person is doomed to spiritual death. You cannot survive spiritually as a loner! The loner who goes his own way and disclaims any need of others and yet claims to be led by the Spirit, is a fake!

When people meet you or me, is the best they can say, "Yes, I suppose he or she is right?" Are the cords of human kindness not visible? Is there no warmth coming out? The pens of inspiration, whether in the Bible or in the writings of Ellen White, speak very strongly: "He whose heart is not imbued with love for God and for his fellow men is not a disciple of Christ. . . . Without love his faith would be worthless" (Ellen G. White, *Testimonies for the Church*, 5:168).

Then Paul opens his heart and says, "I will show you the most excellent way." And the first point he makes is that love is patient. This has to do with being able to take the things that are being thrown at you by somebody else without losing your composure or temper. Life is not fair; it can be very cruel. Things will be laid at your door that do not belong there. It is unjust and it is unfair, but it is what we all sometimes have to meet—it is life. Says Paul, Love can take it without being thrown off course. The one who is being wronged has it within his or her reach to avenge himself or herself, but chooses not to. Love makes a man or a woman slow to anger. And that is a sign of strength. Love is strong.

Love is kind. This is the positive counterpart to patience: Love is good not just at taking things as they come, but goes out of its way to show kindness even to those whom one finds a constant trial and whose behavior is unacceptable. And there are a fair number of such individuals around. The kindness of Christianity contains what Origen called the capacity to be "sweet to all."

Love does not envy. There is a mean streak in envy. It is humanly impossible to have feelings of envy toward another person without looking for ways of discrediting, downgrading, and possibly destroying the other person. And the closer a community is linked together the more are the opportunities to compare ourselves with others. The Adventist Church is such a community. And we are also an achievement-conscious community. The ones who don't succeed are often made to stand out. And we end up creating an environment for envy.

Love does not boast, it is not proud, and it is not rude. Praising yourself or focusing on your own accomplishments is pretty useless. If you are really all that good, why not let others say it? Love finds no satisfaction in self-glorification. And particularly as one looks to Christ, who, when all is said and done, is the only One worth looking at, one begins to discover that the greatest joys come from the deepest humility.

When you truly love someone the love you have for that other person is not seen as a favor you bestow on the one loved. The true sentiment of a real lover is the sense of wonder at the fact that someone loves you in an unqualified manner. The greatest discovery in life that anybody can make is to discover that somebody loves you! And that somehow you cannot find enough to return to match what you have received.

The experience of Mary Magdalene when she came with the costly ointment to anoint the feet of Jesus tells us something about how love behaves:

1. Love has a built-in spontaneous dimension of extravagance

and generosity. Love does not ask how much it will cost. It just gives all, and regrets that it has no more to give.

2. Mary had sinned much and had received forgiveness for it all. An unqualified love and devotion to the Master was all she could offer in return, but no one was going to stop her in expressing that love.

And so I look at this in wonder, I who have also been forgiven much by my Lord, who rescued me from my moments of waywardness and loved deeply, and I ask myself, "What have I brought to my Master?" I have so little, and yet I love Him so much!

Love does not seek its own; it is not selfish. Self-interest is not its agenda, and therefore it is rightly considered super-human. It is of God. Love is prepared to give up for the sake of others even what it is entitled to. It is a different mind-set. Remember the appeal of John F. Kennedy in the halcyon days of hopes and dreams, and would-be-Camelot, "Ask not what your country can do for you, but what you can do for your country!" Now loving in this manner and giving of ourselves is a huge thing. It is difficult, and it runs counter to what we basically are; but could we not make the effort? It is a better way to live life when we think less of our rights and more of our duties and responsibilities.

Love is not touchy; it is not prickly; it is not easily provoked to anger. Oh, how easy this is to say but how difficult to live. Do you remember the hurt you saw in the eyes of that child or spouse, who loves you so much, after you lost your cool and resorted to abusive language? Love is unsuspecting; it is immediately prepared to place the most favorable interpretation on the motives and acts of others. It does not look for the seamy and unfavorable explanations, and it does not listen eagerly for the unkind rumors and reports. Generosity is the hallmark of love.

Love does not keep score of wrongs. The notion, "I will forgive, but I will not forget" is a myth if that means we cannot be done with the past. I know there are scars that will remain with us for life, but they are only a reminder of our journey, where we have been, and what we have left behind. They must not be allowed to mar our life as we begin a new day. Love helps us to move beyond what happened yesterday.

Lord, someone let me down today; I was upset and
I said harsh things.
It is so easy to be superior when other people make
mistakes;
To wag the finger, to shake the head,
As if I never made a mistake, never let anyone down.
Lord, forgive me for my lack of understanding
Lord, help me to show the same mercy to others
That I would wish for myself.
Lord, preserve me from any desire for revenge
Stop me from ever trying to get my own back.
Help me to give to others
The forgiving love I continually receive from you
(Frank Topping, *Pause for Thought*, pp. 172, 173).

This is my prayer:
Lord, You have given us immense power and freedom
Above all the power and freedom to choose to reject
love coming from You or another person.
Help me to choose a loving way of living,
For only love can change the things that matter.
Only love can change people, for love is at the heart
of creation.
True love comes from You, O Lord
You have shown us its meaning.
Thank You, O Lord.

CHAPTER TWELVE

THE CERTAINTY OF HIS COMING

More than two thousand years have passed since Jesus said, "I am going to prepare a place for you, and I am coming back to take you there. Trust Me" (see John 14:1-3). And for two thousand years the believers have trusted Him, and continue to do so. The believers know the promises, and they know that He who made them is trustworthy. The believers also understand that the second coming of our Lord signals the beginning of the final acts by which God will bring His created universe back to the original design in creation—that of perfect harmony between God and His creation. But the passing of time causes the believer to ask: Why is it taking so long?

Living next to the believers are the scoffers who challenge the life of faith, and whose intent is to make it all seem an illusion. They contemptuously dismiss the hope of the believers and ask: " 'Where is this "coming" he promised? Ever since our fathers died, everything goes on as it has since the beginning of creation' " (2 Peter 3:4). It says of them that they "deliberately forget" (verse 5). This suggests that their "forgetting" is more serious than just a moment's lapse of concentration; it is a *choice* they have made. But, says Peter to the believers, "You must not forget. The Lord is not slow in keeping His promise. In the interest of salvation He is just patient."

There was absolutely no doubt among the first generation of believers that Jesus would return and that history was moving toward that climax. It is also very clear that you cannot be a believer in the tradition of the early church without also believing that Jesus Christ will come again. The gospel itself would be incomplete without either Christ's first or second coming (see Ellen G. White, *Christ's Object Lessons,* pp. 227, 228). The belief that Christ will come again shaped the lives, values, and choices of the early believers, as it must do ours. The apostle wrote: "[That reality] teaches us to say 'No' to ungodliness and worldly passions, and to live self-controlled, upright and godly lives . . . while we wait for the blessed hope —the glorious appearing of our great God and Savior, Jesus Christ" (Titus 2:12, 13).

In the inspired messages from God and in the age-old Christian tradition the question is not whether He will come back, but, rather, how to prepare for it, and how to live with a clear sense of certainty, urgency, and readiness. The "thief in the night" symbolism used to describe the second coming of our Lord (see 1 Thessalonians 5:2-4; 2 Peter 3:10; Matthew 24:42-44) tells us that there will be elements of surprise and of the unexpected in His second coming when it does happen. In the parable of the ten virgins (see Matthew 25) who were awaiting the arrival of the bridegroom, they were to stay awake with lamps trimmed and full of oil. Alas, they all dozed off, and five ran out of oil. In this Jesus taught something about both the suddenness of His coming and the frame of mind that must characterize those who live in expectation of His coming. We are told to stay awake, to be alert, and to live ordered and sober lives (1 Peter 4:7; 5:8; 2 Peter 3:17). But to many that is not easy. Life is sometimes treacherous, and one can feel very alone; and at times it all seems more than one can bear. I am reminded of the old fisherman's prayer:

"Dear Lord, be good to me,

The sea is so large and my boat is so small."

And then there are the aches we carry—in our ailing bodies and hurting hearts; and we ask, maybe with some anxiety: "How long, O Lord? What else must happen?" The events of life are sometimes more than we think we can cope with—the cup seems so full.

Says the Lord, It will not be long, but I will give you some signs along the way (see Luke 21:9-11; 2 Timothy 3:1-4) both to help you remember My promises, and to help you recognize the passing of time and the lateness of the hour.

Under the stress of unresolved questions, with which we sometimes torment ourselves, our human mind can play tricks on us. One may, for a few fleeting moments, wonder whether He who said that "you do not know the day or the hour" is waiting simply to test our endurance, to see who will stay the course, who will stay awake and who will fall asleep, to discover who will disqualify themselves along the way by disclosing signs of unworthiness. We may wonder if such "delay" as there is, is brought on by these concerns. Is this compatible with the all-loving God we have come to know? I think not. To present such a picture would be an unjust and sinister caricature of God. God's primary concern is to save as many as He possibly can. The One who so loved the world that He gave His only Son so that no one should perish, is "patient with you," desiring "everyone to come to repentance" (2 Peter 3:9). *That* is His ultimate concern, and the passing of time must be understood in that context.

Even so, the question keeps coming back: Why so long? We see sufferings, the reports and images on television will not go away, and we have our own painful personal experiences. We see wars and all possible natural disasters; it is as though the whole creation cries out, "It is enough! It is enough!" Is it not?

Even as we ponder the difficult questions, painful as they are, we must remember that with our human limitations we can understand only a little; we see through "a glass darkly" only the outlines of God's design, and reasons that are clear to Him may be a mystery to us. Therefore, Jesus said, " 'It is not for you to know the times or dates the Father has set by his own authority' " (Acts 1:7). The decision about when the hour is right rests ultimately in the sovereignty of God. It is not given men to know with certainty *when,* only with certainty that it will happen. And that certainty creates an urgency that each generation of believers sustains and lives with. Only then does one make the right choices in terms of values, priorities, and commitment.

As we contemplate His promises, the fire that burns inside us is a longing for the Lord to come quickly. From time to time, in earnestness and sincerity, we ask ourselves: Can I do anything to hasten His coming? Am I a hindrance to its happening? What can I do?

In searching for answers to these questions we may become too inward looking and supply answers that, although they contain some truth, may not be as helpful to our spiritual journey as we think. Some may be inclined to look mainly at their own spiritual short-comings and conclude that the reason for the delay is that we are not personally ready. Our priorities are not right. We are not gaining enough victories. We are not good enough! (Are we ever?) The indifferent spirit of Laodicea and the rebellious spirit of Kadesh-Barnea are still so dominant among God's people. And we are mindful of the words from the pen of inspiration that "it is the unbelief, the worldliness, lack of consecration, and strife among the Lord's professed people that have kept us in this world of sin and sorrow so many years" (Ellen G. White, *Selected Messages,* 1:69). And as we look at our church and ourselves we are only too aware of the fact that we are nowhere near the model that Christ had in mind for His church as a community "without stain or wrinkle . . . but holy and blameless" (Ephesians 5:27). And we have to confess that we are not living the kind of "devout and dedicated lives" (2 Peter 3:11, NEB) that Christ expects of believers who live in anticipation of His coming. And the truth is that many who "profess to have the oil of grace in their vessels with their lamps, have not become burning and shining lights in the world" (Ellen G. White, *Maranatha,* p. 55).

Yes, these realities cannot be denied. The church fails so often to be what the Lord expects His people to be. We fail in love, and we fail in service. And most of the time we know it. Surely there is something we can do about it!

While it is right and proper that each of us examine ourselves and seriously address our own situation, it is not right, as sometimes happens, that in lamenting our personal shortcomings, we find occasions to begin examining each other, and begin to point out and address perceived shortcomings in the lives of other people. When that happens, the spiritual climate in the church chills significantly. The church community quickly becomes an unattractive place, and the people there become unlovable and unloving. None of us is doing so well or is well enough placed to be the spiritual judge of our fellow travelers. Spiritual shortcomings are personal and are most often best addressed on a personal basis.

We said above that the final decision about *when* the hour for the Lord's return has come lies hidden in the sovereignty of God. That is a decision He has reserved for Himself to make. Yet God has given to mankind some insight into the goals and objectives He is seeking to accomplish before He comes that may serve as pointers.

First, Peter reminds us that "the Lord is not slow in keeping his promise, as some understand slowness. He is patient with you, not wanting anyone to perish, but everyone to come to repentance" (2 Peter 3:9). God's intent is to save as many as He possibly can. In that respect His work is not yet finished The message of Jesus that the end will not come until the gospel of salvation is presented as a witness to all peoples (see Matthew 24:14), although the achievement of that is not easily measured, nevertheless underlines the wonderful truth that our Savior is not going to close the door prematurely. Throughout eternity no one shall have cause to say, particularly looking for someone who is not there, "Could You not have waited a bit longer? Could You not have tried a bit harder?" Our Savior will have done all that can be done; and He will not return until that is so. That is the way His mission of love and redemption moves Him. But obviously there comes the moment when also He will have to say, "We have done what we can. Let us now close this painful chapter of human history."

But the timing of that decision is hidden in the sovereign wisdom of God. And only the all-knowing God can measure the depth and extent to which His offer of salvation in Jesus Christ has been communicated to all. When one remembers God's commitment to the salvation of men and women, the passing of time becomes an element of reassurance rather than threat to our certainty of His coming. Such waiting as there may be is for very good reasons. "Bear in mind that our Lord's patience means salvation" (2 Peter 3:15). We want Him to come

117

quickly. And yet, as we look around and as names and faces flash before us, we are painfully troubled by the absence of someone we had hoped would be there. Maybe He should wait a bit longer? The Lord knows our agony.

Second, as we search for answers to our questions, we accept, however difficult it may be to fully understand, that there are reasons for God's allowing rebellion to run its course. When Jesus Christ returns He will return as the victorious One who will not be challenged again because He has delivered the final and full answer to the challenges of Satan. Nothing will have been left unresolved. No further answer to the sin problem will be needed.

The father of rebellion, who introduced sin into the hearts and lives of our first parents (see Genesis 3) by suggesting to them that God was less than truthful and that His motives were suspect, will at the return of Jesus Christ have lost all credibility. Satan will have had time and space to demonstrate through wars, human sufferings of exploitation and deprivation, illnesses and death, what the consequences of rebellion against God are. He will have had time to discredit himself. In His sovereign wisdom God knows that He must allow time and space for sin and rebellion to run its course. Painful, yes, but with a view to eternity, there is no other way. Our loving and caring heavenly Father must make sure that when the hour comes that He is able to respond to our cries for deliverance, rebellion against God will never again be an attractive option.

Therein lies our only guarantee for eternity. "Every question of truth and error in the long-standing controversy has now been made plain . . . Satan's own works have condemned him" (Ellen G. White, *The Great Controversy,* p. 670).

If rebellion against God does not arise a second time, it will not be because we lack the freedom to choose to go contrary to God's plan, should we so wish, but because having once been set free from the curse of sin, we and the universe will never again want to be trapped in it. Rebellion will have been totally discredited. Its attraction is gone forever. The history of sin will stand as the most convincing witness against itself.

For the "act" to be finished, time and space are needed. We are living in that time today. The course of rebellion against God is well advanced in its process of discrediting itself. Even so, only God knows when time is up.

It is clear that in God's final and ultimate answer to the sin problem there are issues to be taken into account that are wider and larger than my personal salvation. For us individually the matter of personal salvation is clearly of critical importance. But for the larger picture, namely for the eternal security of the new creation and its inhabitants, God will also have provided a far-reaching answer that deals with the roots as well as the consequences of rebellion.

Without Christ's return the controversy between good and evil cannot be brought to an end. Without His return God's design both in creation and salvation cannot be realized. Without His second coming all His promises will fail to find their fulfillment. There is no future without the Second Advent; redemption cannot be completed. Therefore, the injunction: "The Lord is soon coming. Talk it, pray it, believe it. Make it a part of the life." (Ellen G. White, *Testimonies for the Church,* 7:237). The whole idea of "Eden restored" (Ellen G. White, *The Great Controversy,* p. 648) signifies the completion of the circle, and God will have brought creation back to His original design. His return signifies the end to suffering. His return means I will meet again my loved one whom I laid to rest a little while ago. His return means that the power of sin that has ruined the life of someone dear to me will be broken. All pain will end. It cannot happen without His return.

How long will it yet be to wait? We do not know; but He has told us to be sober, to watch and pray, and to keep an eye on

119

the "fig tree," i.e., be sensitive to the signs of the times as we move through history.

The fact remains that I cannot be a believer without also believing in the second coming of our Lord. If, somehow, there is no room for that thought in my plans, then my faith rests on something other than the Word of God. To the true believer the Second Coming is the fulfillment of one's deepest longings— the moment when all we have hoped and lived for meets us. To the world that has gone astray, the second coming of Christ is bad news; to the believer it is the ultimate moment of joy.

Said our Lord: " 'Behold, I am coming soon! My reward is with me.' . . . The Spirit and the bride say, 'Come!' And let him who hears say, 'Come!' Whoever is thirsty, let him come; and whoever wishes, let him take the free gift of the water of life" (Revelation 22:12, 17).

And as we go through life and experience joys and disappointments, we are buoyed up by the certainty that faith brings and find the strength to live through moments of anxiety. We keep our eyes fixed on Him who was, who is, and who shall come again. He can be trusted. He knows how to keep His children safe.

I said to the man who stood at the gate of the year:
"Give me a light that I may tread safely into the unknown."
And he replied: "Go out into the darkness and put your hand into the hand of God. That shall be better than a light and safer than a known way."*

---

*Inscribed outside George VI's chapel in Windsor, England.

INTERVIEW WITH JAN PAULSEN

Q. What are the main tasks of the General Conference President?

Paulsen: As General Conference President, one has to remember—I have to remember—that my assignment is a spiritual one. I am not the chief executive officer of a corporation. It's a spiritual leadership role that I have. Yes, there are executive functions, executive decisions that have to be made. Monies have to be spent. Decisions about personnel and programs and buildings and what-not—they have to be made all the time. But all of this finds its meaning in the kind of community we are as a church. That is, as a mission instrument in the hand of God. So I am probably more conscious on a day-to-day basis of that than I am of anything else in regard to my work assignment. The fact is I am a team leader for a community with a mission entrusted to us by God and whether we achieve and accomplish what God has in mind is defined entirely by how we perform in mission.

Q. What do you bring from past experience?

Paulsen: I suppose I consider myself somewhat fortunate because I come from a very broad international background in the church. I have lived in Europe for many years. I have lived in Africa, and now in North America. I have served for almost half of my professional life in the educational community. I have been in field ministry and in administration—both college administration and division administration, and now here at the General Conference. So this varied background has, I think, prepared me for what I am now doing. I think it would be difficult for me if I had not had the kind of background I've had—not least my international experience.

Q. From your vantage point, what do you think are the church's strengths at the moment?

Paulsen: It is very clear to me that the Seventh-day Adventist Church was God's idea. We are here because God caused this movement to arise, and we have a very specific mission to do. That is very clear to me. I see the hand of God in the life of the church—constantly at work. The church as a community created by, empowered by, and given the agenda by God is to me a very, very real thing. It is not a hope. It is not a prayer. It is a present reality. I am very conscious of that and sensitive to that.

In that sense I feel that the church's strength at this time lies in the fact that we are, as a church, being very deliberate about our mission. We use our resources as we plan strategically and financially. We make plans which are driven by the mission of the church. It's the mission that drives our decisions. It's a very deliberate, a very conscious stance we've taken. Let the mission given to us determine what we do and how we spend our monies and in what order we undertake our programs. And if we cannot define a particular series of activities or initiatives, if we cannot define it within the mission agenda of the church, then we shouldn't do it. We should leave it. And that gives an enormous strength to the church. I see the church growing very rapidly as a result, I think, of the resolute commitment that we are here to finish the work in these last days so let's get on with the task.

Q. Do you see the size in some way becoming a liability?

Paulsen: I see it very clearly as a strength in the sense that when you are small, when you are young, when you are a little fellow, you are easily intimidated, and the world out there is a big place. And there are forces at work and at play that can be very intimidating for a spiritual community that is very small. As we have grown and are growing in size, as we now work in 200-plus countries of the world, and as the Adventist family—I mean the whole family, children and all—is somewhere round about twenty million and growing at a tune of about one-and-a-half million a year, there are many out there who are saying: This is a big community. We'd better be aware of them. We'd better talk to them. We'd better be sure that we keep some level of consultation and communication going. I see that as a strength because the church can in this way be a voice, be a factor for change in many ways. Change for the good also in society if these influences are exercised in a proper manner. I think we can be a significant voice addressing religious liberty and freedom of conscience on the international platform, at the United Nations, or whatever. I think we can be that. I see, therefore, the expanding community as a strengthened hand. As long as we remember that we have no independence in that sense, that we function separately from God. As long as we don't begin to think of ourselves as something great, then I think we can be strong.

123

A liability? Maybe not a liability, but a challenge also that as the church grows rapidly around the world, you have to be very, very deliberate and very conscious of the need to work to hold this family together, so it doesn't fragment or begin to think in terms of "we are big enough in our little corner—we can decide everything as we wish here," that we don't need to defer to anyone else. That's a challenge.

Q. Do you see particular ways that you can facilitate the church working together as one when it's this size?

Paulsen: Because of our internationality, our church is so diverse. By diversity I mean not just race, I mean culture, I mean habits, experience. The whole spectrum of human encounters, human experience has many faces to it. So we as a church carry that broadness with us as a diverse international community.

Yes, we have to be deliberate in regard to what we do. We have to be very conscious of the decisions we make and to try to make room for the fact that the church which is international needs to have opportunity to express its internationalism. We are not a church of one particular locale or one particular cultural flavor. We are not. And we must allow space for that to happen without compromising our fundamental identity, because our identity as a church is cross-cultural, cross-racial.

Q. What about some weaknesses? Do you see things that are difficult for us right now?

Paulsen: What did the writer say? "We have nothing to fear for the future lest we forget how He has led us in the past"? Weaknesses show up when we forget whence we've come and why we're here.

Looked at from the point of a human administrator, yes, I wish we had more resources. We're always overextended, and it's because we are so preoccupied with mission. Every time we vote a budget at the General Conference, it's a statement of faith in the people, because the people haven't failed us so far. From the point of human administration I wish we had access to a lot more resources.

But then, of course, I remember that silver and gold and the cattle upon a thousand hills, you know, are His.

Q. Can you think of challenges that we're going to have to deal with in the future?

Paulsen: It's such a difficult question to answer without creating symbols and signs and challenges which may not be there, so it's a difficult one to answer. Obviously there are matters in my own mind and in the minds of my colleagues that we are conscious of and working with, but I think for us it is a matter of being alert and focused.

I'm reluctant to begin to make a list of challenges which are in some way graded. I do think that if I can speak more generally, I think the main challenges we face are the challenges of rapid growth and of unity, and I mean by that that all elements of our church, every local congregation remembers that we are part of something which spans the whole world, and we do not live unto ourselves.

Q. So one of the challenges is to keep all of us reminded of being part of the family?

Paulsen: Yes, and to nurture that which binds us together. Paul in Ephesus speaks of the bond of unity which the Spirit brings. To look after these things, that is a big challenge.

I think it is also, if I could move to something else and maybe identify one or two other things, I think one of the very big challenges we face, which we must succeed at, is in allowing or empowering the younger generation of Seventh-day Adventists to take charge of the church. They are not just foot soldiers. They are men and women of ideas—creative ideas, and I'm thinking here of the young men and women, young professionals, and students. They are critical to the future of the church. I want to encourage them to assert their strength of involvement in the church.

Then I think we need to do rather better at demonstrating an inclusiveness in the services of the church which give creative roles also to women. We have some distance to go with that.

Q. What do you enjoy most about the job that you have right now?

Paulsen: I think maybe the fact that it gives me an opportunity to minister to the whole international church of God. The fact that I, from my particular vantage point of ministry and service, can feel the pulse of a church that spans the whole globe. It gives me a wonderful sense of joy and fulfillment to see the strength of the family and to discover even when I go where I cannot understand what they say, a dynamic that defies definition, which says we are part of the same family.

Q. How is your family adapting to this role?

Paulsen: My wife is and has been a wonderful partner. She doesn't enjoy the best of health physically, but she has a wonderfully strong mind, a creative mind, and she is a very active participant in my own thought life and is therefore invaluable to me. So I feel that she blends in with what we are doing here in Washington. My children, regrettably, are scattered, and that is, I suppose, one of the prices one pays of a life of international service. So I have right at this moment a daughter in England, a son in Oslo, and another son in Rwanda in Africa. Maybe two years from now it will not look quite the same again. My children have been very supportive of what Kari and I have been asked to do. Very supportive.

Q. It is not an easy balance to keep, right? It's a demanding job.

Paulsen: Yes. There is never a time, never a day, when you are not the president. Therefore there is nothing called a holiday when you can entirely disengage from the office you serve. If you cannot take that, you shouldn't do the job. So you are within reach all the time by telephone and email, and you have to be reachable. But I would say this, that I am surrounded by some very wonderfully strong and creative colleagues, and they carry a lot of the responsibilities at the General Conference.

Q. Have there been times in your life when there was dramatic evidence of God intervening over these years?

Paulsen: Oh, I suppose going back to our service in Africa in the mid-sixties. Nigeria, the Biafran War, and being then principal of the college. I had responsibility for students who came from Biafra and was trying to look after their security and safety. And in some instances even driving a minivan with mothers and babies to the Niger River and getting them across to the eastern side of the river. The risks you had to take—being stopped on the road by soldiers of the opposite forces and not knowing how exactly this was going to end, soldiers who were so under the sway of palm wine that it was difficult to relate. I had instances in that conflict where it was clear to me that God was holding a hand over me and my ministry. Very clear to me that He was holding my hand.

I feel also that in some of the hardships that have come to my family, an accident to my own son, and my communications with the Lord in that connection. I felt many times that the Lord talked to me and reassured me that He understands and that He is there, that He is not going to leave me. It's a wonderful sense of God's presence in moments of great anguish and many of these have come to me during my service.

Q. Could you talk about your prayer life for a moment?

Paulsen: It is in the sense that like every other person, I

127

belong to the human race. I am as affected by the Fall as anyone else, and I have a lot of growing I need to do. And the Lord is not finished with me yet in that respect. So I need to talk to Him every day about myself. I have to be brutally honest with Him, with myself, and with the other issues that need some refinement in my own development, in my own growth. So I think it is fair to say, it sounds very selfish, but in my own private devotional thoughts and life, I think first of myself.

My wife and I talk about these things and we pray together daily when I am home. But it does deal with my own issues and then placed on top of that comes the responsibility that God has given to me in my work and there is no end to the elements that I need to talk to Him about.

I feel also that I am talking to the Lord about the things that I should prepare in my sermons. I prepare my own sermons. I don't use anyone else to write my sermons, so I need to know what the Lord wants me to impress upon the people, to have some sort of sense that this would be good for the church, for the people I am going to talk to, to take up.

So these are things that come through in my prayer life. Then I pray for my family. The Lord is wonderfully caring. We may love our own kids a lot. It's good for me to know that He loves them more than I do, and that gives me a lot of strength. Also I would say that there are very few things which give me a greater lift than when I travel around and somebody who is a total stranger to me—I mean I have never met them—they come up to me and say to me, "I want you to know, pastor, that every day I mention you by name in prayer to the Lord." No one knows what that does to me, to think that people who are otherwise strangers to me take the trouble to mention me or my family by name to the Lord in prayer. It is a wonderful experience.

128